live
work
and play
around the
world

live work and play around the world

SHARYN McCULLUM

Kangaroo Press

DISCLAIMER The author has tried her utmost to ensure the information in this travel guide is the most up-to-date available at the time of going to press, but things can change (sometimes too rapidly), and neither the author nor the publisher can take responsibility for this.

Any organisations mentioned are listed in alphabetical order. Their listing does not constitute recommendation by the author and publisher.

The author and publisher cannot take responsibility for any losses incurred by transactions on the Internet. It is up to the individual to confirm the website is secure before sending any private details and payment.

LIVE, WORK AND PLAY AROUND THE WORLD
First published in Australia in 2000 by Kangaroo Press
An imprint of Simon & Schuster (Australia) Pty Limited
20 Barcoo Street, East Roseville NSW 2069
A Viacom Company
Sydney New York London Toronto Tokyo Singapore
© Sharyn McCullum 2000
All rights reserved. No part of this publication may be reproduced, stored in a retrieval system, or transmitted, in any form or by any means, electronic, mechanical, photocopying, recording or otherwise, without the prior permission of the publisher in writing.

National Library of Australia Cataloguing-in-Publication data:

McCullum, Sharyn.
Live, work and play around the world.
Includes index.
ISBN 0 7318 0830 4.
1. Employment in foreign countries - Directories.
2. Travel - Guidebooks. I. Title.
910.202

Cover design: Gayna Murphy, Greendot Design
Internal design: Gayna Murphy, Greendot Design
Set in Garamond 10.5/12.5
Printed in in Australia by McPherson's Printing Group.

10 9 8 7 6 5 4 3 2 1

SHARYN McCULLUM has been travelling all her life, thanks to a father who worked for an airline.

In 1988 she ventured overseas on her first working holiday. This trip, and subsequent trips, have inspired her *Live, Work and Play* series of travel guides.

To keep the information up-to-date Sharyn travels regularly, and uses her established network of contacts throughout the world.

Sharyn is happy to hear from readers, employment contacts and associated travel services who can offer information to improve the guide for future fellow travellers. Please send any correspondence via email to: **sharynmccullum@hotmail.com**

Look out for the *Live, Work and Play* website: **www.liveworkplay.net**

BY THE SAME AUTHOR:
Live, Work and Play in London and the UK
Live, Work and Play in Australia

The author would like to thank all those people who gave their time and knowledge freely, and even those who felt the extraction of information was like having a tooth pulled.

SPECIAL THANKS TO:
Peter Alcorn for his help with the Internet
Dearne, James, Matthew and Jordan Alcorn
Philip Ruth
Travellers' Medical Vaccination Centre, Sydney
(www.tmvc.com.au)
Department of Foreign Affairs & Trade (www.dfat.gov.au)
Gus Zalami and MH Matrix

Contents

Introduction 9

PART ONE

Chapter 1: Ready, Set, Go! 2
Passport 2
Visas 3
When to go 5
The question of money 6
Holiday insurance and medical care 9
Useful things to do, obtain and join 12
Packing 17
Checklist—let the countdown begin 24

Chapter 2: Departing and Arriving 26
Departing and arriving by air 26
Departing and arriving at land borders and sea crossings 29
Duty-free, protected and heritage items 29
Getting into town 29
Taking care of formalities once you have arrived 30

Chapter 3: Accommodation 31
Should you pre-book accommodation? 31
Short-term accommodation 32
Long-term accommodation 32

Chapter 4: Travel 38
Should you pre-purchase your travel? 38
Travel options 39
Country/area travel options 49
Africa 50
The Antarctic 52
Australia 53
Canada 55
Central and South America 57
Egypt and Israel 59
Europe, Scandinavia and
  the Commonwealth of Independent States 60

Indian subcontinent 63
Japan 64
New Zealand 64
The Oceans 66
South-East Asia and China 67
United Kingdom and Republic of Ireland 69
United States of America 72
Travel alone 74
Travel safe 75
Travel well 77
Live, Work and Play's budget travel tips 81

PART TWO

Work around the world map 82

Chapter 5: Work 84
Working holiday schemes 84
Programs 85
Sponsorship 89
Securing cash work after your arrival 89
Options for finding work 91
Should you organise work before you go? 96
A quick word on tax obligations 97
About the employment contacts listed 98
The Australia/New Zealand/South Africa and
    United Kingdom/Republic of Ireland connection 98

Chapter 6: Area Analysis 99
Africa 99
Australia 100
Canada 105
The Caribbean 106
Central and South America 107
Eastern Europe and the Commonwealth of Independent States 109
European Union and European Economic Area 109
Republic of Ireland 112
Israel 112
Japan 116
The Mediterranean 119
The Middle East 119
New Zealand 121
South-East Asia and China 122
United Kingdom 123
United States of America 128

Chapter 7: A–Z of Jobs 131
Accounting, banking and financial services 131
Agriculture and farming 134
Allied health (including nursing) 141
Care work 145
Cargo/freighter ship positions 146
Cruise-line positions 146
Equine staff 149
Freelance journalism and photography 150
Holiday camps 150
Hospitality 153
Information technology 158
Nanny, mother's help and au pair positions 159
Non-mainstream work 165
Office support 167
Retail 169
Ski centres 170
Teaching 174
Technical, industrial, trades and general labouring 180
Tourism 182
Translators 184
Volunteer work and programs 184
Yacht crewing 187

Index 190

Introduction

So you want to live, work and play around the world? Whether this be for a few months, a few years, in one country or a number of countries, you have come to the right place to jump-start your travels.

It would be really nice if we could jump on a plane to a foreign country and live, work and play to our heart's content! Unfortunately, there are harsh realities to contend with, such as visa restrictions. The goods news is that there are working holiday schemes and programs available that allow you to experience life in another country for an extended period.

There are several factors that spur people to leave their comfort zone and travel overseas into the unknown. Some people agree that disillusionment with life prompts them to go, while broken romances are another major reason. Some people are lucky enough to be transferred overseas. Others like the thought of listing overseas companies on their curriculum vitae. For some, it is just something they've always wanted to do. Others simply want to experience foreign cultures and meet people before they 'settle down'.

Whatever your motivation for wanting to live, work and play around the world, you don't need to be a gregarious child of adventure to do so. All you need is a passport, a visa, a desire to experience new cultures, the will to take any work available and a penchant to have fun—well, that's my theory anyway!

While some people can just get up and go, there are those who plan their trips well in advance and/or in minute detail. Some people can even require a lot of reassurance to get them going. Whatever you are, nervous first-timer or seasoned traveller, treat this travel guide as your friend, a friend who will reveal secrets and other things to you that only a friend who has lived, worked and played extensively around the world can, and will, do.

The philosophy of this friend is to lay out on the table up-to-date, practical, comprehensive and relevant information on living, working and playing around the world. A lot of the information is based on first-hand experience and knowledge, not only from myself, but from fellow travellers, professional organisations and employers.

Unfortunately, many travellers arrive overseas and find themselves with no friends, no family, no work, nowhere to live, and wondering: What do I do now? Through this friend, most of your worries and concerns (and those of family and friends) should be alleviated. After all, that's what friends are for!

This guide has been divided into two parts. The first half has four chapters containing pertinent travel-related information which will help you to prepare for your trip and aid you once you are on the road. The first chapter, Ready, Set, Go!, will help you to organise yourself before you go. Departing and Arriving will give you the lowdown on countries' departure and arrival procedures. The Accommodation chapter discusses the pros and cons of the many accommodation alternatives. And the Travel chapter advises you not only about options to travel the world but offers advice on travelling well, safe and alone.

The second half of this guide is totally devoted to work opportunities around the world and is divided into three chapters. There is a general work section which provides specific details on working holiday schemes and programs, along with suggested ways of finding work before and during your travels. The Area Analysis chapter provides an overview of work opportunities available in different countries—and there are many of them, which is good news for us. There is then an extensive alphabetical listing of work options along the way. Each profiled work opportunity is backed up with suggestions on how to gain such work. Many employment contacts are listed, which should make finding work that little bit easier.

The contact details in both parts are listed in alphabetical order (for easy reference) and not in any order of preference of myself or the publisher. The contact details not only include street addresses, telephone and fax numbers, but website addresses, making this guide extremely Internet-friendly. And when you contact any companies mentioned here, please let them know you saw their details in this guide.

Once you have looked at both parts, it is then up to you to decide what information and work contacts are relevant to you. With a little added follow-up research and preparation on your part, you will have a head start to putting your travel desires into action.

Thousands head off on working holidays every year. Right at this very moment someone is packing their bag! And soon, you will be joining them. So read on, and live, work and play.

Sharyn McCullum

PART ONE

CHAPTER 1

Ready, Set, Go!

PASSPORT

A **passport** authenticates your identity and is required to enter other countries. So, if you don't have one already, you had better get yourself one. Most passports issued are valid for 10 years. If you already have one, check the expiry date. It is wise to have one that is valid for some time (a couple of years at least) just in case you decide to extend your trip from a few months to a few years.

There are also many countries (e.g. Indonesia, Singapore, some African countries, Malaysia) which stipulate that passports must be valid for at least six months before they will issue a visa or allow entry into their country (this is in case you are detained in the country through circumstance or illness). People with passports that had less than six months before expiry have been refused entry, so check your passport's expiry date.

It can be a hassle having to apply for a new passport while travelling. This is because you will most likely need to ring home to obtain documentation to support your application. You will also need to support yourself while the passport is being processed (the length of time required can vary and may take up to a few weeks), so it is preferable to organise a new passport before you go.

If you, your parents or grandparents were born in another country or you marry someone from another country, you may be eligible for a passport from that country.

Holding passports from two countries is referred to as **dual nationality**. For example, if you have heritage from a European Union (EU) country, you may be eligible for an EU passport. Having one of these will allow you to live, work and move freely throughout EU member countries.

EU member countries are Austria, Belgium, Denmark, Finland, France, Germany, Greece, the Republic of Ireland, Italy, Luxembourg, the Netherlands, Portugal, Spain, Sweden and the United Kingdom. Iceland and Norway haven't joined the EU, but are part of the European Economic Area (EEA), and citizens from these countries can also live, work and move freely throughout EU member countries. For more information on the EU and the EEA, refer to the 'European Union and European Economic Area' section in Chapter 6 or visit the EU website at www.europa.eu.int

Although dual nationality has the advantage of allowing you to live, work and play in that country, disadvantages may arise. For example, some countries require their citizens to undertake military service. If you missed the 'call-up', immigration officials may consider you a *defaulter* and imprison you. Therefore, before applying for such a passport, establish your military service status from the Embassy or Consulate. If you decide to apply for one, obtain written confirmation (both in English and the language of that country) that you are exempt from military service. Always travel with this exemption so that you can show immigration officials if required to.

VISAS

A visa is an endorsement stamped in your passport which allows you to enter another country. There are a variety of visas available, including tourist visas, multiple entry visas, transit visas, business visas, work permits, student visas and working holiday visas.

This guide is chiefly concerned with working holiday schemes and work programs. There are a number of countries that make working holiday visas available. For an overview of working holiday visas and work programs see Chapter 5.

It is *your responsibility* to make sure you have the *appropriate visa* in your passport *before* entering a country. It is worth noting that you do not have to apply for a visa in your own country but you can apply in other countries while travelling. You will need to find out how long the visa will take to be issued so you can organise accommodation during this waiting period.

Although travellers like to collect stamps in their passport from many countries, it is worth finding out whether a visa in your passport from one country will make it difficult to enter another; e.g. an Israeli visa makes your passport invalid for travel to Islamic countries except Jordan, Egypt, Turkey and the United Arab Emirates. I would ask the issuing Consulate if it is possible for the 'offending' visa to be given on a piece of paper separate from your passport.

Visa regulations are subject to change and revision, so it is highly advised that you contact the appropriate High Commission or Consulate of the country or countries you intend to visit for the latest details. Do note that in some cases you can download the information, including application forms, from the Internet.

What if I don't qualify for a working holiday visa or program?

Working holiday schemes and programs are usually aimed at young people between the ages of 18 and 30. What if you don't qualify?

- Teach English. Being qualified to teach English will allow you to work in many countries around the world, because many language schools will sponsor you to work for them. Refer to the 'Teaching English' section in Chapter 7.
- Work on a cruise liner. Cruise lines prefer to hire people who have qualifications and a number of years' experience. Thus, a large proportion of staff are over the working holiday and program age limits. Refer to the 'Cruise-line positions' section in Chapter 7.
- Ask the Embassy or Consulate of the country you want to work in if there is a shortage in particular professions. If there is, and you specialise in this area, then this could improve your chances of having a work permit approved.
- Find a program. Some programs, such as being a camp counselor (this is the American spelling), in the USA, do take on those over the normal age. Refer to the 'Holiday camps' section in Chapter 7.
- Kibbutz programs are becoming open-age. Refer to the 'Israel' section in Chapter 6.
- Become a volunteer. Offering your services as a volunteer is a way to experience another culture and to help a community or individuals. Refer to the 'Volunteer work and programs' section in Chapter 7.
- Trade your services for accommodation and food. Refer to the 'Non-mainstream work' section in Chapter 7.
- Look for cash work. Being paid in cash often means you do not have the appropriate paperwork to be working legally. If you do find cash-paid work during your travels, do note that you are at the mercy of your employer. You will have no rights and will not be able to complain if you are unhappy about the working conditions and pay rates. If you feel ripped off, you will either have to put up or shut up.
- Gain sponsorship from an employer. This can be a long, drawn-out process.
- Be transferred with work. There are many international companies which allow you to be transferred to work in one of their overseas offices, so if you currently work for such a company, ask about these opportunities.

- Study. Student visas are available to those undertaking full-time study (or learning a language) in another country. Under the terms of the student visa you are usually allowed to do part-time work. Some people who find they like a particular country sometimes apply to study in that country so they can stay.
- Consult an immigration specialist. An immigration specialist may be able to offer you some legal alternatives.
- Look into dual nationality (see above).
- Have a working holiday in your own country.

WHEN TO GO

Any time is a good time to begin your travels, although there are some factors to keep in mind:
- your savings—need I say more?;
- the seasons—you may wish to avoid some seasons, for example the rainy or mid-summer seasons, and if you are not a 'cold-weather person', try to arrive during the warmer months (warmer months can also yield an increase in work opportunities as workers take their annual vacations and temporaries are required to fill their shoes; at the same time, accommodation prices can skyrocket, with the main tourist spots becoming overcrowded);
- the availability of a particular type of work, which can be influenced by the seasons (e.g. hospitality work increases during summer and ski positions during winter)—under the various headings in the Work chapter I have tried to indicate the busy and quiet times for work;
- the cost of airfares and accommodation—travel during off-peak seasons rather than peak seasons as prices are lower; some people prefer to leave as close as possible to the end of the low season, which allows them to get a cheaper airfare *and* arrive at the beginning of the next season—but book early if you are going to travel during the low season, as many people could be looking to do so as well.
- your currency's exchange rate;
- special events—sometimes the importance of attending an event should take precedence over factors like the cost of an airfare and accommodation (is saving a couple of hundred dollars worth it if you miss something you really want to see?);
- school and public holidays;
- the time taken to obtain your passport and appropriate visas.

The choice is yours, but if you just want to go, then just go.

THE QUESTION OF MONEY
How much to take

'The heaviest baggage for a traveller is an empty purse.' So take as much money as possible. Though you may hear stories of travellers arriving with no funds to their name, and landing on their feet, this is not recommended. The more money you have, the more freedom of choice you have. The amount you need will vary from country to country as some are more expensive than others.

To qualify for working holiday visas you need to prove you have a certain amount of funds to support yourself for the initial months of your stay; e.g. Australians are required to have A$4500 and New Zealanders are required to have NZ$6000 in a bank account before they can apply for a UK working holiday visa.

If you are spending time travelling before you arrive at the place you want to work in, then you will need to budget for accommodation, food, local travel, sightseeing and spending money during this period. Alternatively, you could pick up casual work along the way. If you have a pre-organised position in another country with a wage and accommodation included, find out when your first pay cheque or salary credit is, because you will need funds until then.

If you're planning to find long-term accommodation, you will need to give the landlord one month's rent in advance and one month's bond/deposit/key money before you move in. Then you may need to connect the gas, electricity, water and phone. You will need to budget for these things. See Chapter 3 for more information.

A QUICK WORD ON FOREIGN EXCHANGE
If your currency is low against other currencies' travel with only a small amount of your destination's currency and travel predominantly with your own currency. Then you can change the rest of your currency if or when the exchange rate improves.

If you are planning to work, you will be paid in the currency of the country you are working in, so you can save the currency you have taken, because you will use your salary. Some travellers have made money on the exchange rate and gone home with a profit. You may possibly want to consider sending money home to capitalise on some exchange-rate movements.

How to take it

There are quite a few options for taking your money overseas. **Travellers' cheques** are popular because if they are lost or stolen the issuing company will replace them. If cash is lost, it is lost.

Thomas Cook and American Express travellers' cheques are the most popular. You can obtain the cheques directly from one of their offices or through most banks. Do obtain a list of commission-free offices and banks to cash your cheques.

The cheques can be issued in a number of different denominations, and it is wise to travel with a variety.

Most companies will advise you to carry cheques in the currency of the country you will be visiting. If you are visiting many countries, you may elect to travel with US dollars as this currency is accepted worldwide. British pounds are also accepted around the world except in the USA.

The good old **credit card**, that fantastic piece of plastic, is extensively accepted around the world. Visa and MasterCard are the most widely accepted cards, and many travellers use them in a variety of ways. Apart from purchasing goods and services with them, you can use them to obtain cash from one of the many ATMs (automatic teller machines) around the world. Remember to find out how much the bank charges for this service before you leave.

Some people deposit cash to their credit card as this allows them direct access to their own money and means not having to worry about paying the monthly bill. This works well until you have used all of your credit and your card becomes a normal credit card again. How will the bills be paid? Refer to 'Sort your affairs' in this chapter for advice on this.

A credit card can also be used overseas to obtain cash advances in the local currency. Note that any transactions made on your credit card in a foreign currency will be converted to the currency of the country your credit card was issued in.

Take note of emergency contact numbers just in case your travellers' cheques or credit card/s are lost or stolen. Many credit cards have frequent flyer schemes, so the more you use them, the more points you will accumulate. You may want to look into purchasing a prepaid, PIN-protected card which will allow you to withdraw cash in local currencies around the world. One such card is Visa TravelMoney which you can purchase from Thomas Cook.

Accessing your **current bank account** around the world is now possible through ATMs which display such signs as Cirrus, Maestro and Plus. Just use your current ATM (cash) card to obtain the local currency. Ask your current bank if they have information on this service and whether EFTPOS (Electronic Funds Transfer at Point of Sale) is also available. Also find out what, if any, bank charges there are for using this facility. It can be expensive.

Before they leave home, some people **open a bank account** in the country they will be spending the most time in. This is because some banks in other countries require two references from you before they will open an account. As you will not have a credit rating in that country, the bank may refuse to open an account. Speak to your local bank to see if they can open an account overseas for you. You may wish to contact Thomas Cook who also offers this service.

When carrying **cash** be aware that some countries have a limit as to how much you can take in and out. Also, some countries require you to exchange money into the local currency or declare the amount of cash you are carrying to customs officials on arrival. If this is the case, definitely insist that the customs official records and issues a certificate stating the correct amount. This can be presented when you leave. There have been cases where this certificate has not been produced and funds have been confiscated at the point of exit.

Do spend all your coins, if possible, because you can't exchange them into another currency. Only paper notes can be exchanged, and even then, foreign-exchange agencies don't like to change notes if they are small denominations.

Changing money into another currency will inevitably incur a commission charge, often about one per cent. The best rates are found at banks, then money changers, such as Thomas Cook and American Express. Hotels can change money for you, but usually their commission is much higher than the banks'. If someone approaches you on the street offering to change money, be careful. Although you may be offered a better rate than the bank, inside the outer layer of rolled-up bills may be currency from another country. Changing money on the black market is illegal and if you are ripped off you have no recourse to complain to local authorities.

If you run out of money, you can have **funds transferred** to you. Banks will do it if you are one of their customers, and Thomas Cook, American Express and Western Union all have money-wiring services. Contact them for more details and any costs involved.

For the options on how to carry your money overseas, consult your bank or a foreign-exchange specialist such as Thomas Cook or American Express, which have other money services available.

Personally, I would carry money in a number of ways. I say this because a friend credited her credit card with all her money, then a rogue ATM decided to 'munch' her card on a Friday night. She had to wait all weekend to retrieve it from the bank on Monday morning. She had no other money available and was lucky friends were able to help her out over the weekend.

Do find out about what currency is appropriate to carry in the country or countries you will be travelling in. For instance, if you are touring east and southern Africa, US dollars and British pounds are accepted. If you are taking your credit and ATM cards, note that only some major African cities accept credit cards and/or have ATMs.

HOLIDAY INSURANCE AND MEDICAL CARE

Accidents happen. Take out adequate insurance for those unexpected mishaps.

Insurance policies can be a drag to read, particularly the fine print. If, however, you are serious about being adequately covered, then a little time spent reading the policy will be worth it.

Your travel insurance should cover you for such things as:
- cancellation fees and lost deposits incurred by unforeseen circumstances which require you to cancel your trip;
- overseas medical, dental and emergency expenses;
- emergency flight home if required;
- missed connections;
- hijack and kidnap;
- loss, theft or damage to your luggage;
- travel delay;
- accidental death;
- loss of income;
- personal liability;
- legal costs.

Here are some things you should check:
- Is there a 24-hour telephone number you can use anywhere in the world in case you need assistance?
- Can the policy be extended for longer than 12 months if you decide to stay longer overseas?
- Are pre-existing medical conditions covered?
- Are goods you buy along the way covered?
- Will the policy cover personal items stolen from a hire car or from accommodation?
- Can you make a claim while overseas or do you have to wait until you return home?

Make sure that your policy covers you for specific activities such as white-water rafting, scuba diving, ocean sailing, winter sports, parachuting and mountaineering if you plan to do them. Also, if you are going to ski, does your insurance cover you for piste closure when there isn't enough snow?

Holiday insurance means just that—insurance that covers you while on holiday. If you are planning a working holiday, check whether the policy covers you for this, and if not, find one that does.

If you are taking expensive items like cameras, video equipment and computers, you might wish to take out additional insurance as these items aren't usually covered in general policies.

Do take emergency contact numbers in case something does happen. Should you need to put in a claim, you should report your loss to the police, hotel owner, and so on, and obtain a written statement on official letterhead (showing their contact details if they are required to be contacted) to back up your story. For medical incidents, obtain a receipt and letter from the doctor for your claim.

It is wise to shop around for holiday insurance. You will find that travel agents will recommend a particular insurance policy. This is because they are aligned with the insurers, and the travel agent will most likely receive a hefty commission if you take out that policy.

Do read the fine print on different policies. Compare how much each insurance company will pay if things go wrong. Although you can't predict which incidents might happen to you during your travels, there is nothing worse than finding out after the incident that your insurance does not cover you for it. Therefore, if taking out holiday insurance be covered for as much as possible.

Some countries have **reciprocal medical arrangements**, e.g. Australia has reciprocal agreements with Finland, the Republic of Ireland, Italy, Malta, the Netherlands, New Zealand, Sweden and the United Kingdom. This means you are entitled to necessary medical and public hospital treatment similar to that offered by Medicare for the duration of your stay in that country. People visiting Australia from these countries receive similar treatment to that in their country. European Union and European Economic Area member states have a special medical agreement. You should carry with you the E111 certificate which entitles you to state emergency treatment.

Contact your government-run health scheme for information on any reciprocal medical agreements. Do travel with details about your health scheme and if you need treatment, ask to be treated under the reciprocal health agreement.

Some people from countries with a reciprocal health agreement often take out holiday insurance to cover them only while they are travelling to another country. If they require any medical assistance, they rely on the reciprocal medical agreement. Then, when they travel again they take out insurance to cover them for that period of travel. The major difference with purchasing holiday insurance in another country is with repatriation. If you were injured, for example, you would be repatriated to the country where the insurance was bought, and not to your home country.

Travel agents and governments will advise against doing the above because they say you should be adequately insured for your entire stay overseas. You will need to weigh up what the reciprocal agreements cover against what the travel insurance covers. If anything did happen and you weren't covered, it could be very expensive for you. And, leaving aside medical matters, you will not be covered for stolen or lost goods if you have no travel insurance.

There are private health schemes in many countries. If you are staying long enough in one country, you may wish to obtain an international transfer from your current private health scheme. This should state your current level of cover and allow you to join a scheme in the new country. The new fund may waive any waiting period because you have this transfer. You should be able to suspend your current private health insurance without losing your benefits, but check with your scheme for exact details.

Medical check-up

Have a **check-up** with your doctor and dentist before you leave as it is horrible being sick in a foreign country.

While at your doctor, obtain enough medication to last you for your entire stay as brands differ from country to country. In third-world countries, medicine may not be what it claims to be. Medicine in those countries can also be stored incorrectly so by the time it reaches you, it has lost its effectiveness or passed its expiry date.

Also, certain drugs which are legal in one country may be illegal in another. Make sure you have a letter from your doctor stating what any drugs you are carrying are used for. It may be worthwhile to have the doctor's letter translated into the language or languages of the countries you will be visiting.

A few years ago an Australian girl was jailed in Greece for having prescribed codeine tablets on her. You might want to ring the relevant Embassy or Consulate to find out if your particular medication will be legal in that country.

If you need ongoing treatment for an existing condition, you should ask for a referral from your doctor, physiotherapist, chiropractor, etc. This should briefly state your condition and what treatment you have been receiving, so when you see a professional in another country, you won't have to send home for vital information. Do take prescriptions for glasses and contact lenses with you.

For information on vaccinations, jetlag, an STD (sexually transmitted disease)-free holiday, and travelling well in general, refer to the 'Travel well' section in Chapter 4.

USEFUL THINGS TO DO, OBTAIN AND JOIN

Sort your affairs

Take the hassle out of paying bills at home by adding an extra signature to your bank account. This allows another person to operate your account on your behalf. If you run out of money overseas, this person will be able to access your account and wire you funds.

You could arrange with your bank to have any bills, mortgages, personal and/or student loans, etc., paid by direct debit, though you must have enough funds in the account to cover these transactions. Also find out about Internet banking. Accessing your bank account via the Internet will allow you to check balances, pay bills and transfer funds from wherever you are in the world, and at any time. You will have total control over your bank details while travelling.

Alternatively, you could sign a **power of attorney** giving a trusted friend, family member or a professional person authority to act on your behalf with regard to your affairs while you are away. Forms can be purchased from legal stationers and some newsagents, and the arrangement is valid until revoked.

As Katherine Mansfield said: 'Whenever I prepare for a journey I prepare as though for death. Should I never return, all is in order. This is what life has taught me.'

Making a will might be unpleasant and sound absurd but it is a good idea. You are going away to enjoy yourself and sometimes you will do things you would not normally do. There is nothing worse than leaving your relatives to sort out the legal mess. Chances are slim that anything will happen to you, but you never know!

If you are from a country that requires you to vote, find out the procedures involved so you can vote overseas if necessary.

International Driver's Licence

You don't necessarily need an **International Driver's Licence** to drive in other countries as most will accept your current driver's licence. However, check with your nearest motoring organisation.

Be aware that in some countries after a certain period, usually after one year of residency, you are required to exchange your current licence for a licence from that country.

If you ride a motorbike or drive heavy vehicles, check if you are required to have an international licence to ride and drive these vehicles overseas. They may be needed if you find work as a motorbike courier or a coach driver for a tour company.

Discount cards

There are international identity cards available to full-time students, teachers or those under the age of 26. These identity cards entitle you to a number of discounts and benefits in some 90 countries.

For full-time students there is the **International Student Identity Card (ISIC)**, which entitles the bearer to discounts on travel, accommodation, museum entrance fees, etc. To obtain this card you need to prove that you are enrolled in full-time study.

If you are a teacher, you can apply for the **International Teacher Identity Card (ITIC)**, which enables you to receive discounts on travel, accommodation, museum entrance fees, etc.

If you are 25 years old or younger and not a full-time student, you can apply for the **International Youth Travel Card (IYTC)**, which enables you to receive discounts on travel, accommodation, museum entrance fees, etc. These identity cards are available at a number of student and youth travel agencies including STA Travel, Campus Travel, Travel Cuts and USIT Travel.

For more information and a full listing of where these cards can be purchased, have a look at the **International Student Travel Confederation (ISTC)** website at www.istc.org

Stay in touch

VIA EMAIL

Email is fast becoming the cheapest and most efficient way to stay in touch with family and friends while travelling. Simply set up a free account with an email service provider, pop into an Internet cafe, access your account and retrieve your email. If you want to chat to someone at home, organise a time to meet them in a chat room.

Do make sure you log out of your email address. It's possible for unscrupulous extortionists to pretend to be you and send email to your family and friends saying such things as, 'I am running out of money, please send some more to this account.' The account, of course, is the extortionist's which they quickly close after taking the funds. Other instances have seen a ransom demand sent via email for money for someone's release.

Most of the travel clubs mentioned in this guide under the 'Australia' and 'United Kingdom' sections in Chapter 6 offer an email

service when you join. Alternatively, you can set up a free email address on the World Wide Web through one of the following:
Hotmail: www.hotmail.com
Rocketmail: www.rocketmail.com
Yahoo: www.yahoo.com

VIA POST

If you want to give people an address to contact you, they can send mail to the old faithful Poste Restante, which will hold mail for you for up to four weeks. Make sure you take ID with you when you pick it up. If your mail cannot be found, check if they have filed it under your first name. An address example would be:

Sharyn McCullum
Poste Restante
GPO Sydney
Australia

Some companies such as American Express have a mail-holding service. So do the travel clubs which are mentioned under Australia and the United Kingdom in Chapter 6.

VIA TELEPHONE

There are a number of ways of keeping in touch by telephone, including direct dial and reverse-charge calls. Whatever method you use, try to make calls in cheaper, off-peak times, and ensure that time differences don't see you dragging a friend or relative out of bed. An alternative to standing in the phone booth pumping coins into the phone is to purchase a **prepaid phonecard.** You can also buy ones that can be 'recharged' using your credit card.

Some phonecards allow voicemail, which work like an answer phone. You call in every so often to retrieve any messages. Contact the telephone companies about these cards.

TRAVELLING WITH A MOBILE PHONE AND/OR A PAGER

If you own a mobile phone, contact your local network for advice about taking the phone overseas. Most networks offer a 'roaming' service which lets you use your phone in other countries. Before you get too excited though, check on the phone charges. Will you be charged at local call rates? Will there be surcharges? If there are, it may be too expensive to take your current phone with you.

If you plan on spending a lot of time in one country, you could always buy a mobile phone once you get there, then, when you are leaving, you could sell the phone to another traveller.

An alternative to using a mobile phone would be to purchase a pager and have any messages paged to you through a message service. Another alternative is to contact mobile phone companies as many now rent mobiles.

Join the National Trust

The National Trust is designed to manage and sustain properties of significance to the public. These can include bush tracks to places and buildings of historic interest.

Usually by joining the National Trust in your own country you get free entry to National Trust properties in other countries.

Some countries require volunteers to help maintain properties. Refer to 'Conservation programs' in the 'Volunteer work and programs' section in Chapter 7.

The National Trust
Australia	*Tel: (02) 6239 5222*
Japan	Tel: (03) 3214 2633
United Kingdom	Tel: (020) 7222 9251
USA	Tel: (0202) 588 6000

Research your destination/s

Travellers who have done some homework on their destination will often get more out of their travels. You will have a head start in knowing about custom 'do's and taboos' involving protocol, body language or hand gestures, appropriate clothing, gift-giving, the use of business cards, etc. You will also have a better idea about what places you particularly want to see and what things you want to do.

So visit or contact tourist authorities for information. Pick up travel brochures from travel agents. Borrow a book from the library or purchase a travel guide. Look in the travel sections of major newspapers and motoring organisations. Also look at travel magazines. Surf the Net for up-to-date information. There are sites for airlines, tour operators, hotels, car rental companies, country and area tourist bureaus, accommodation, travel products, travel medicine, etc.

Join travel clubs

Travel clubs throughout the world provide many services, including: booking your travel; providing information for accommodation and employment; mail-holding service (very useful when you don't have a permanent address); fax service; luggage storage (very useful if you need to store accumulated possessions); phonecard and

voicemail; email; providing computers so you can type your CV or surf the Net; tax-return service. They are listed under relevant countries in the Area Analysis chapter in Part Two. These include:
- Australia: Global Travel Team, ITAS and Travellers Contact Point;
- United Kingdom: the Backpacker Co., Deckers London Club, Drifters, Global Travel Team and London Walkabout Club.

Join frequent flyer schemes

Most airlines are linking their frequent flyer schemes with other airlines, car rental companies, hotels and financial institutions. By continually using these services you should build up your points to receive free flights and other goodies in the future.

Sort your work documents

If you intend to seek work through agencies or by approaching companies directly you will need a current **curriculum vitae** (CV). This should be no longer than three pages (you will lose people's attention if it is any longer, and first impressions count) and should include:

Personal details—include your name; full and current contact details (including email); your date of birth; and nationality.

Education—list the schools and universities you have attended as well as the grades and any qualifications you have obtained and what year you obtained these.

Employment history—begin with your most recent job first. Give a brief description of the job, including your duties and responsibilities and your reason for leaving.

Referee details—in many countries it is a legal requirement that two references must be provided and checked by the agency or employer before a position may be offered. Employers like to see the original copies of these. Include all referee contact details as it is nothing these days for employers to call the other side of the world to confirm references. If a friend is writing a reference for you or you are putting their name and contact details to a reference, make sure you let them know about this in case they receive a phone call.

Personal interests—a brief spiel about your interests.

It is becoming law in several countries that those working with children provide a **written criminal clearance**. I also found this necessary for teaching in the UK, and some medical positions. It would be very helpful for those considering work in these areas to obtain a written criminal clearance from their local police.

Employment agencies like to sight **original qualifications, certificates**, etc. If you do not have originals, make sure your copies are notarised or certified by somebody authorised to do so or by the professional body which issued the document or documents.

You may wish to have your documents laminated so they travel better and are not torn or crumpled.

Prepare yourself

Although not a prerequisite, you may wish to obtain extra skills to enhance your chances of gaining work while travelling: learn to sail or dive; undertake a bar course; gain a qualification or experience in child care; obtain a life-saving certificate; obtain licences to ride a motorbike or drive a truck or bus; gain a coaching/instructing certificate in tennis, soccer, skiing, water sports, etc.; learn how to make a cappuccino, a flat white and espresso coffee; take a typing course or a computer course.

Get fit! (though you should get fit while travelling!)

If you are worried about not speaking the language then you may wish to learn some useful words and phrases before you arrive. I have found that at least learning to say 'hello', 'goodbye', 'how much?', 'thank you' and 'f— off' have proved useful.

PACKING

Firstly, let me say, there are no set rules to packing. OK, now I've said that, packing is an arduous task at the best of times; trying to squeeze in everything you think you will need for an extended stay overseas can be horrendous.

Before you begin to pack you need to **choose suitable luggage**. Now before you go out and spend hundreds on new luggage, have a look at what you already have. It seems that a lot of new travellers think they should go out and purchase the latest gear just because they are going overseas. They seem to forget there are stores overseas where you can purchase appropriate luggage at a later date.

Backpacks or travel packs are a good bet, but if this isn't your style, at least get something that is easy to carry. Ask yourself what kind of travelling you think you may do—independent travel using bus or train passes, etc., or organised touring? If you are choosing more independent travel, please note that not all accommodation is near the train or coach terminals and you may find yourself walking a long distance to that hostel a traveller recommended. Plus, not all terminals have luggage storage facilities, so it's a must to have luggage that is easy to carry. It is often easy to spot a new, inexperienced traveller by the brand-new, heavy luggage they are dragging ... er ... carrying.

Choosing a backpack

Spend time seeing what various backpack designs have to offer.

Size can play a major role. New travellers are notorious for filling their luggage with clothes they *might* wear and knick-knacks they *might* use, and thus purchase the largest pack possible. Big is not always the best. The bigger the pack, the more likely you are to over-pack and end up with a hernia. An experienced traveller's tip is therefore to buy a smaller pack.

Most packs are measured by their litre capacity which, if you're like me, doesn't mean very much at all. A visual evaluation will be your best bet on judging the size you want and require.

As not everyone is the same height or size, you should definitely try on the pack. The only thing worse than a heavy pack is an uncomfortable, heavy pack. Your pack should fit you like a glove because the more comfortable you are the better you travel.

As well as being the right length, the pack's straps should be adjustable and be able to be stored in a compartment in the pack. Most packs have straps and handles enabling you to carry them either horizontally like a suitcase or vertically on your back.

Some packs are top-opening while others have zippers and open like a suitcase (you'll know what I mean when you see them). I prefer zipper-opening ones as I have seen people with top-opening ones having to dig deep or unpack belongings to find what they are looking for. For instance, while waiting in a queue to buy a Tube ticket in London, the backpacker in front of me wanted to buy a student ticket and needed his student ID, but where was his ID? You guessed it—oh dear, at the bottom of his pack.

Many packs come with a detachable daypack which will be handy for overnight stays and carry-on luggage for the plane. These also come with extra features such as toiletry bags, but it is up to you to decide whether or not you would use such features and whether it is worth paying for features you may never use.

The quality of the pack will often determine its strength and sturdiness. In particular, a lot of strain is exerted on the zip area. A pack with a heavy-duty zip that is lockable is a good investment because the last thing you want is to find your pack has split its seams.

Packs vary in price so you will need to shop around at travel gear specialists, luggage stores, camping and disposal stores.

If you decide to stick with a suitcase, invest in one which has wheels, or purchase a suitcase trolley to help your bag glide along.

If you don't buy a backpack with a detachable daypack, you will need a small **daypack** or **carry bag** for the plane to hold your camera, Walkman, diary, etc. This could also double as luggage for overnight or weekend trips.

For those contemplating work in an office, some kind of bag besides your daypack will be handy. I know when I see someone in corporate dress with a daypack, I think, yep, you're probably a working holidaymaker and you may have all your valuables in that bag. This would be attractive to thieves.

Don't forget to label your luggage, inside and out. Also have locks for every zipper, and maybe personalise your luggage—with a ribbon or sticker—so it can't be mistaken for someone else's.

Once you have luggage you can consider what to pack. Ask yourself these questions: How can I avoid looking like a tourist? What countries am I travelling to? Will these countries have dress regulations? When am I arriving—summer or winter? What work clothes will I need? Will I need to take my own work tools?

OK, so here's how not to look like a tourist. Professional thieves prey on unsuspecting travellers who are easily identifiable carrying luggage, and may be carrying valuables. Of course, you will be seen at some stage with your luggage so try to find a place to store your gear as soon as possible. A friend once said, 'I dress down because people seem to leave me alone that way.' I have found this comment true in my travels and you too can take this into consideration when packing. Don't dress like you have loads of money and don't wear the family jewels unless you are going to a ball at the palace.

Some people advertise where they are from by wearing T-shirts with emblems of their country plastered all over them. This, or wearing a T-shirt purchased on holidays, may prove to be a sign of wealth in some countries and you may be harassed. It could also say: 'I'm on holiday and I have loads of money to spend. I'm also carrying a camera and other expensive items which, if you're a thief, you should steal.' So don't advertise you are a tourist, try to blend in. On the other hand, T-shirts can be sought-after items in some countries, and thus a good bargaining tool to swap for indigenous items.

Check if there are any customs related to dress. For instance, in Turkey, women are required to keep their legs and heads covered when inside mosques. If you do not adhere to dress regulations you will be stared at, and I've even seen friends spat at.

You will need to pack for all types of weather—swimwear for summer, an overcoat for winter, plus everything else in between. Wear layers, then you can peel them off when hot and pile them on when cold. Take items that are appropriate to your trip. For example, if trekking, you will need good walking boots.

You will need work clothes that suit the type of work you intend doing, e.g. if you are hoping to find bar work, pack a white shirt and a black skirt or black pair of pants, or if you are going to work in an office, pack corporate attire. I have included specific clothing requirements under each work opportunity in the Work chapter.

Dark colours are a good investment—they don't show the dirt as much when travelling. This is important as you may not always have the opportunity to wash them on the road. Clothes that are versatile, comfortable, not too bulky and low maintenance (easy to wash, quick to dry and/or don't need to be ironed) are good.

Going on holidays usually means you want to buy new things to take with you; this can deplete your savings for your trip. Save your money for shopping expeditions to buy local products.

If you intend setting up home somewhere, you might be thinking of taking your own sheets, plates, and so on, but keep in mind that many travellers either find fully- or partly-furnished accommodation or rent furniture for the duration of their stay. Depending on the type of travel you may be doing, a plastic plate and a knife and fork may come in handy (but be wary at borders as any type of knife may be misconstrued as a weapon).

Some people like to take a little comfort from home, and bedding is one item they are particular about. So if you need that pillow or quilt cover, take it, though you can buy these on the road.

All items suggested below are just that, suggestions. Makeshift and old items will do the job just as effectively as new ones. A lot of things can be bought as you need them, so even though it is nice to have new things to take away, save your money for your travels.

Look in charity, church and second-hand shops and go to markets, bazaars and jumble sales for cheaper clothing and items. Good places to look for compact travel items are in disposal and camping stores, bric-a-brac stores, travel agents and bag/luggage shops. Or you can request items as a present, if Christmas or your birthday is coming up, or as a farewell gift.

What to pack—some suggestions

UNDERWEAR
THERMALS For extremely cold climates.
SHORTS One or two pairs.
PLAIN T-SHIRTS
SWIMWEAR For warmer weather.
SUNGLASSES

JEANS One or two pairs.
JUMPERS One or two, preferably long to keep your backside warm; try to avoid bulky ones as they can become cumbersome.
THONGS/JANDALS/FLIP-FLOPS OR SANDALS Very useful to wear to shower blocks in camping grounds and for walking in hot weather.
JOGGERS/HIKING BOOTS/WALKING SHOES One pair with good, thick soles. Wear them in before you leave home so you don't get blisters. If travelling in cold weather, you will be wearing them every day and you need to be comfortable.
SOCKS
GOING-OUT OUTFITS One or two good ones.
GOING-OUT SHOES One pair.
WORK OUTFITS Adapt these to the type of work you hope you will be doing. Refer to the individual work opportunities in Chapter 5.
COAT These can be bulky to carry, so a good, light, waterproof or windproof jacket (preferably with a hood for sudden showers) would be OK. The hood also keeps your head warm.
GLOVES A necessity in winter as chilblains aren't a good look.
HAT/BEANIE Even when you are wrapped up warmly you still lose heat from your head. In summer a broad-brimmed hat or cap keeps the sun off.
SLEEPING BAG/SHEET Very handy for dossing on friends' floors, travelling and staying at hostels (though most hostels provide sheets and blankets, mostly free but some do charge a rental). If travelling to cold climates, you will need one that can withstand very cold weather. Down-filled are the warmest. To save space when packing a suitcase, unroll the sleeping bag and lay it flat across the top of everything else.
MONEY BELT Despite being uncomfortable and making one look pregnant or have a beer gut, this is a safe way to carry money, travellers' cheques, tickets and other valuables. You could buy one that you wear around the neck or maybe invest in a bum bag. If you find these uncomfortable, as many do, then you can be innovative and hide valuables in your underwear or socks, or sew hidden compartments into your clothes.
TORCH Preferably a small one. You will be surprised at how often this comes in handy.
TRAVEL CLOTHES LINE AND PEGS It is hard to find a clothes hoist when you need one.

WASHING POWDER Tubes of liquid wash are available from supermarkets and travel agents. Large hostels usually have washing facilities where you can purchase a cup of soap.

PLASTIC BAGS To hold dirty washing and stuff. Good to wear over socks if ever caught without waterproof shoes.

WALKMAN AND FAVOURITE TAPES Leave tape covers behind to save space; keep tapes together in a bag. A player that records as well as plays means you can send tapes home.

CAMERA AND FILM

TRAVEL IRON Handy if you take clothes that need ironing.

COATHANGERS A couple are useful.

TRAVEL CLOCK You don't want to be late for work now do you? If it has a loud tick, take the batteries out, otherwise it could be mistaken for a bomb at airports or border crossings.

POWER-POINT ADAPTOR Duty-free shops carry sets of plugs for different areas of the world. The prongs vary from country to country, so a set of adaptors is very useful if you are taking a hair dryer or electric shaver.

FOLDAWAY UMBRELLA This can be bulky to carry. A waterproof jacket is more versatile.

PASSPORT PHOTOS You will need these when applying for some visas. Some employment agencies like them to be attached to CVs and you may require one for travel passes.

SWISS ARMY KNIFE

REPAIR KIT: NEEDLE, THREAD, SCISSORS Take small scissors only, so you don't set off any metal-detector alarms. It's so embarrassing!

INSECT REPELLENT AND/OR PORTABLE MOSQUITO NET

TOWEL/S Take a chamois towel rather than the traditional type.

HAND TOWEL For long journeys when you need to freshen up. It feels much better than paper towelling or toilet paper.

TOILETRIES Buy travel-sized items, like roll-on deodorant instead of a large can, or two-in-one shampoo and conditioner. You can always revert later. Note that aerosol cans can explode in your luggage from the pressure in a plane's luggage-hold.

TOILETRY BAG Preferably waterproof and with handles so you can hang it up on hooks in the shower. Or use a plastic bag.

PLUG Not always provided in shower blocks. If you like to shave or wash your face in a basin, take one.

TOILET ROLL Don't laugh, you will notice that a lot of countries do not supply toilet paper in public toilets.

BANK REFERENCE You may need one of these to open a bank account in another country.
PERSONAL REFERENCES Some landlords require them for long-term accommodation as do employment agencies.
TRAVEL DIARY For all those wonderful memories.
ADDRESS BOOK To keep in contact with old friends and to add new ones.
WRITING MATERIAL Prepaid aerograms are available at post offices.
MULTI-VITAMINS In case you drink too much and don't eat properly.
CONDOMS A necessity these days.
FIRST-AID KIT Constipation, diarrhoea and upset tummy tablets, bandaids (plasters), headache tablets, travel sickness tablets, eyedrops, nasal spray, medicated ointment, etc.
WATER BOTTLE/WATER PURIFIER/WATER PURIFYING TABLETS
SUNSCREEN The sun does have a bite in many parts of the world.

OK, you have chosen your luggage and gathered everything to take, now lay it all out on the floor to see what you have. Get a cup of coffee or tea or your favourite potion then sit in front of your piles and consider why you're taking each item. Convince yourself of its worth or worthlessness. Finally, let's pack.

Everyone has a trick for packing. One method I find useful is rolling clothes up tightly, which minimises wrinkles and lets me fit more in. I've also found that packing heavy objects in the middle, close to the back of the pack, helps keep the centre of gravity in the right place. Keep useful accessories and things you will be needing frequently near the top for easy access. Better still, keep them in a daypack. Remember the student backpacker at the Tube station?

Also, keep in mind any baggage allowances on planes and organised trips. This is usually 20 kg. Some airlines have a size and weight limit on cabin luggage so check this out with your travel agent.

In order to minimise weight, get rid of unnecessary packaging. Take new shirts and pantyhose out of boxes. A friend of mine uses empty spice jars and film cases to carry enough toiletries to get her to her destination. She also carries money and jewellery in them. I collect the sample sachets of shampoo and conditioner delivered in the post or given away free in magazines.

I dare you to do the luggage test. Now that you are packed, take it for a walk. How far did you get? If not very far, how will you manage overseas? It's back to the drawing board with your packing! Get rid of those 'just in case' items.

If you find you can't fit everything in or are over the 20 kg airline allowance and you believe you can't live without all your essentials, you might consider sending some luggage as unaccompanied baggage. Ring your airline's cargo department and find out rates and procedures. Or contact a shipping company about sending a tea chest. But try to travel as light as possible—it makes life a lot easier.

Remember to keep something out to wear on the plane, something comfortable and loose fitting, and suitable for the weather at your destination. If arriving during colder months, carry your coat on the plane with you and have it hung up.

I suggest that you dress nicely when travelling by plane, particularly through countries with strict drug laws, as I have found people of scruffy appearance are often singled out to be searched. I had an experience leaving Bangkok after a three-day stopover. I was with six others who had all been on the same stopover. I wore shorts and a T-shirt to the airport (it was around 40ºC). I was the only one whose luggage was searched.

You might wish to have some activities for the plane: books, music, games, pack of cards, etc. Check with the airline if you can use computers and CD players as they can interfere with navigation equipment. Mobile phones are specifically banned.

The following items are often useful on long-haul plane travel (and other long-haul trips)—an eye mask; socks to keep your feet warm; earplugs to keep out the engine hum; a face or hand towel and toiletries to freshen up with; a bottle of water spray to keep your face moisturised; a blow-up neck rest; sinus tablets; and a change of underwear. Smokers may like to wear and take nicotine patches.

CHECKLIST—LET THE COUNTDOWN BEGIN

Six to eight months before departure
- ☐ arrange passport
- ☐ apply for visa/s

Two to four months before departure
- ☐ book air ticket and other travel
- ☐ book accommodation
- ☐ vaccinations
- ☐ medical and dental check-up

One to two months before departure
- [ ] confirm travel arrangements
- [ ] pre-book accommodation
- [ ] sign power of attorney
- [ ] make a will
- [ ] sort out finances, arrange travellers' cheques, open an overseas bank account, and make any other financial arrangements
- [ ] obtain an International Driver's Licence
- [ ] join Youth Hostels Association and other clubs
- [ ] obtain ISIC, ITIC or IYTC discount cards
- [ ] set up email address and organise mail holding, etc., and give details to friends and relatives
- [ ] obtain information on your destination/s
- [ ] update CV and obtain all necessary references
- [ ] obtain criminal clearance

Week leading up to your trip
- [ ] at least 72 hours before, confirm your flight
- [ ] farewell family and friends
- [ ] pack and label backpack or suitcase
- [ ] cancel milk and papers
- [ ] arrange care for pets
- [ ] photocopy the front section of your passport, itinerary, insurance policy, airline ticket, etc., and give to a family member or friend in case of emergency
- [ ] take a pen to fill out the landing card
- [ ] organise small denominations of cash for transport and other purposes at the other end
- [ ] purchase duty-free items

Happy organising!

CHAPTER 2

Departing and Arriving

Immigration and customs procedures involved in departing and arriving at airports, seaports and at border crossings in different countries can be rather confusing, even for the initiated.

DEPARTING AND ARRIVING BY AIR
Departing

The first thing to do is to **check in** at the appropriate check-in counter at least 90 minutes before your flight is due to depart. Here the check-in staff will require your passport and ticket (or reference number and identification if booked over the phone or Internet) before issuing you with a boarding pass. Your luggage will be tagged and sent to be loaded onto the aircraft. The corresponding luggage stub/s will be stuck on your ticket which will be your reference if your luggage doesn't arrive at the other end.

Many countries charge you a **departure tax** before they will allow you to leave the country. Some cities such as Sydney charge an Airport Noise Tax. Depending on the country, this tax is collected either by being included in the price of your ticket or by you personally paying the tax at the airport.

Next stop will be the **scanners**. This is where your hand luggage is put through an X-ray machine to check there are no metal objects (like guns or knives) in it. If you are carrying any suspect items, your hand luggage will be searched. If travelling with a laptop computer, ask if it can be examined by hand instead of going through the X-ray machine, which can damage it. This means you will have to turn the computer on to prove to the customs people that it *is* a computer and not a bomb. Sometimes you will be told that the X-ray machine will not damage the computer and it will be put through the machine regardless. You will also be required to walk through a scanner, which will go off if you have metal objects on you.

Next stop, **Immigration**. No matter what country you are leaving, you will need to have your passport handy for immigration officers to check. If you are a national of that country you may be waved through or, in many cases, a departure date stamp will be stamped in your passport. Some countries may require you to fill in a departure card. Have a pen handy.

Once through all the procedures, you head for your **departure gate** to board your plane.

When you buy **duty-free** items at the airport you will be required to pick them up as per duty-free instructions. If you purchased duty-free items in the city, an official at the airport may tear off the appropriate documentation stapled to your goods.

Arriving

Some countries require you to fill in a **landing card**. These are usually handed out on the plane. If not, there will be plenty at the immigration section. There may be other forms like customs and quarantine declarations to be filled in. Do have a pen handy.

On arrival you will follow the signs, or the other passengers, to **Immigration**, where the immigration officers will require your passport, landing card and customs and/or quarantine declaration.

Although you may have the appropriate visa stamped in your passport, immigration officials have been known to give people a hard time when entering some countries. This can be the case when you are entering under a working holiday scheme.

The immigration official can interrogate you on the purpose of your visit. Do stress that the main purpose of your visit is for a holiday, and that any work you might take will be incidental to your holiday and will only be taken to make some money to further your travels. *Do not* ever say, 'I've come to find work' as this statement is not the aim of working holiday schemes.

Officials may ask to see your return airfare or proof you have enough funds to support yourself.

Note: I don't want to horrify you, but there have been instances with Australians and New Zealanders arriving in the UK on an ancestry visa and being required to undergo a full medical examination at the airport before they were allowed to enter (this possibility is mentioned in the information provided with the application form).

The way you act with immigration officials can also be a factor in them deciding your length of stay. Immigration officials have a lot of power, so do not act too cocky even if they are rude to you. Just be polite and answer all their questions.

The way you dress can also influence your entry. Remember my incident leaving Bangkok. Do try and make an effort to look tidy at border crossings even if it only means having a shave, brushing your hair and putting on clean and tidy clothes. Immigration officials can code discreet messages to customs officials, which while we can't interpret, can mean 'search this person'.

Some countries require you to declare the amount of cash you are carrying or require you to exchange your currency into local currency as mentioned in 'The question of money' section in Chapter 1.

There are also countries that require you to list valuable items in your possession, for example, camera, electrical goods, watch and jewellery. You must keep this declaration with you and present it on leaving the country if requested.

Make sure any items that you give to the immigration and customs officials, such as your passport and money declaration, are given back to you. I remember travelling into China with my father and his passport was put into a drawer by an immigration official. My father asked for it back but the official kept saying he did not have it. If my father had not raised hell he would not have got his passport back. I'm sure his passport was intended to be sold on the black market.

Once through Immigration you head to the **Baggage Claim** area to claim your baggage. Some airports have luggage trolleys available for free, while others charge for their use.

Once you have all your luggage, head to **Customs**. Customs usually operates on an honour system with aisles marked 'Nothing to Declare' (usually in green) and 'Goods to Declare' (in red). Sometimes you may need to hand a customs declaration to an official (this is what the immigration official would write his discreet coded message on). Countries belonging to the European Union have an extra aisle marked in blue as there are different duty-free allowances. Be aware of these allowances because if you exceed your allowance you may be required to pay duty.

Keep in mind that if officials find your CV and work references in your luggage, they can take these documents as proof that you will be looking for work at some stage. Even a letter from your parents or friends asking how your job is going or making a reference to your job hunting can be interpreted in the same way. You can be deported if these documents are found in your luggage in a country for which you lack the appropriate working visa.

This has happened to people who have decided to travel through America before reaching their working holiday destination. Even though they have had a working holiday visa for another country, American officials have suspected that they might look for work during their time in America, and have therefore refused them entry. This is why some people join the travel clubs mentioned in this guide so they can send their documents to themselves through the club's mail-holding service. Another option is to email your CV.

DEPARTING AND ARRIVING AT LAND BORDERS AND SEA CROSSINGS

Immigration procedures depend on the type of transport being used. Immigration officials usually board trains to check documents. If travelling by coach, you may be required to leave the vehicle and walk through the border control, or an immigration official may board your coach. If travelling by car, you may have to hand your documents through the car's window to the immigration official.

With sea vessels, immigration procedures vary. If you cross a border by ferry, such as in the Mediterranean and the English Channel, you will have to walk through Immigration at the other side. If you're on an ocean liner, immigration officials may board the vessel and do the paperwork there. If you cross by yacht, officials will either come aboard or you will be required to report to officials within a certain period after arriving.

DUTY-FREE, PROTECTED AND HERITAGE ITEMS

The onus is on you to declare 'suspect' items in your possession. If you do not and are caught carrying illegal items, there are severe penalties, including fines, jail terms and even death sentences.

Do be aware of the duty-free allowances of your final destination. If you go over the set limits, you may be required to pay a duty or have the goods confiscated.

Most countries have strict guidelines on importing and exporting protected wildlife and products which are made from animal bones, animal skin, coral, ivory, etc. So before you purchase that ornament, pair of shoes or handbag, make sure that you will be allowed to take it out of the country and into another one.

Also be careful when you purchase items with heritage value. This category includes books, stamps, coins and artefacts. You may need a special permit to import and export such items.

GETTING INTO TOWN

All airports and seaports are connected to major cities by public transport. Coaches and trains are cheaper than catching a taxi.

Sometimes you can pre-purchase your ticket from your travel agent before you leave home. If not, just follow the transport signs.

Beware of taxi drivers walking around the airport offering you a lift. Make sure before you get into any taxi that you are well aware of how much the fare will be.

If you are on an organised tour or a stopover, find out if a pick-up (transfer) from the airport is included.

TAKING CARE OF FORMALITIES ONCE YOU HAVE ARRIVED

You need to take care of some formalities before you can begin to live, work and play.

In some countries, including Japan and the Republic of Korea, you are required to **register as an alien** with the authorities (either the local police or at the nearest town hall) within a certain time after your arrival. Penalties may be imposed if you do not do so.

If you will be working, you will be required to **apply for a tax number** so that you will be taxed correctly. I have put more detailed information about tax obligations in Chapter 5 and under the individual countries in Chapter 6.

One important early purchase will be a **street directory**, which will have two very important functions. First, it will prove extremely helpful while you are looking for somewhere more long-term to live. Second, it will stop you getting lost on your first day on a new job or when registering for a tax number or as an 'alien'.

Some employers will require you to have a **bank account** into which your salary will be paid. Opening an account can prove traumatic, and depends on the bank you approach, the branch you choose, the teller you happen to get, and the mood he or she is in. Employment agencies themselves will have a banker and can often provide you with an introduction letter making the process of opening an account easier.

CHAPTER 3

Accommodation

There are two purposes to this chapter. First, to give you an idea of what accommodation is available around the world; and second, how to find it.

SHOULD YOU PRE-BOOK ACCOMMODATION?

If you like to know there's a place to go when you arrive, then pre-book some accommodation. You can purchase a 'package deal', which includes airfare and accommodation, from travel agents; some include breakfast. After a long flight, train or coach trip it is hard to predict just how you will feel when you reach your destination. Not all of us can bounce off our transport straight away; you may need somewhere to curl up and recover for a few days. I suggest you pre-book a few days' accommodation (possibly a week or two) as during this time you will want to get over your travel-lag, do some sightseeing, find your bearings, and look for work and long-term accommodation. It's surprising how quickly these first few days go.

See your travel agent for more information on available accommodation. Also visit tourist authorities and look in the travel sections of newspapers and travel and motoring magazines.

If you don't pre-book accommodation, don't fear, you can find somewhere to stay on arrival through accommodation desks in information centres at airports and major train or bus stations. They will ask: What price do you want to pay? What area do you want to stay in? What type of room do you want (single, double, etc.)? Once these are established, suitable accommodation will be found. You will be charged a small booking fee for using such a service.

Sometimes the best accommodation is not what you've pre-booked, but what you stumble upon. While travelling the world you will encounter many types of accommodation—B&Bs (bed and breakfasts), beach huts, villas, capsules, pensions, farm houses, apartments, caravans, home stays, home swaps, cottages, castles—some are indigenous to particular areas and offer a unique experience.

SHORT-TERM ACCOMMODATION
Hostels

Many travellers (of all ages and nationalities) stay in hostels and there are plenty of these around the world. Some are Youth Hostels Association–affiliated while others are independently owned. If you are travelling alone, hostels are a great place to meet other travellers.

Hostels vary in the creature comforts they offer. These days they usually include: personal lockers in rooms; breakfast or a fully equipped, clean kitchen with enough room in the fridge to leave food; a common room; a laundry with coin-operated soap and washing machines and an iron; telephones; a travel booking service; luggage storage facilities; safety deposit boxes; bathrooms that are cleaned daily (some rooms may have an en-suite); lifts (elevators) to all floors; and 24-hour access. Hostels are usually situated in prime sites and are either close to transport or offer a pick-up service. Best of all, they are budget-priced and often have discounts for longer stays.

So with all that's on offer, how do you choose a hostel? Fellow travellers are the best source of advice as they can either recommend or pan a particular place. After all, isn't that what they're for?

Accommodation in hostels is largely dormitory-style (dorm), with a varying number of beds (bunks) in a room. Some hostels now offer a limited number of single, double, twin and family rooms.

The number of occupants per dorm room can vary from four to 12 or more. Some dorms are single-sex, others are mixed. Some hostel owners (not many, but there are a few), only have dollar signs in their eyes. If you don't request a bed in, say, an all-female four-bed dorm, they could put you in an eight-bed mixed dorm. I had that experience in a Darwin hostel. I was the only female sharing with three males. They were very considerate (I was lucky), but one of them did have extremely pungent-smelling walking boots!

Dorm living is an experience if you aren't used to it. You will be sharing with people you don't know, but you'll have a common goal—to travel. Be prepared for people changing in front of you, having little or no privacy, people coming in late and getting up early, zippers zipping, bags rustling, alarms going off, snorers, and even bonkers (who are usually embarrassed in the morning!).

Even though you want budget accommodation, I have met a number of travellers whose health has suffered through too much dorm living. I had one friend who always seemed to have snorers in his dorm and he became crankier and crankier as the days passed from lack of sleep. If this happens to you, then paying a little extra for a good night's sleep in a single room would be worth it.

SECURITY IN HOSTELS
Sometimes it's not professional thieves you have to worry about, but your fellow travellers. Be careful in hostels with your personal belongings, especially your valuables. There are transients who will steal things such as jewellery and cameras, and sell them quickly.

Other popular items to go missing include that expensive shampoo and conditioner you have just bought to revitalise your hair, or that new deodorant, or that carton of milk, or that new T-shirt—some cheap travellers just don't have any regard for other travellers' items and it's sad to say, but that's how they survive.

STAYING HEALTHY IN HOSTELS
As I mentioned before, sleep deprivation is a health hazard. So are bad eating habits.

Hostels usually have a communal kitchen for you to use. Cooking and eating in front of others who aren't eating can make you self-conscious. Maybe you could suggest to your room mates that they join you in going out for a healthy meal. Either that, or you could all prepare, cook and share one. Easy things to cook include pasta dishes—a bag of pasta and a bottle of sauce can be bought easily and cheaply at supermarkets. So can soup and bread.

I know when you are travelling on your own it can be easy to pop into a fast-food shop for a quick bite, but try and eat sensibly.

Types of hostels

YOUTH HOSTELS ASSOCIATION
The Youth Hostels Association (YHA) is known around the world for providing budget accommodation. Being a member of the association gives you access to accommodation in around 70 countries.

The hostels vary in grade, but all have a communal bathroom, a common room and a fully equipped kitchen. Some have a cafeteria providing low-cost meals.

Accommodation is dorm-style, usually about four to a room. There are singles, twins and family rooms available. Each bed has linen, a pillow and blankets. There is a 'book-a-bed-ahead service' which is useful during busy times to ensure a bed is available for your arrival.

Being a YHA member gives you access to a number of discounts on travel, tours, insurance, camping gear, travel guides, etc.

Contact your nearest YHA office for membership details. There are a number of hostel websites on the Internet. Find them by searching for 'youth hostel'. You could call up the International Youth Hostelling site, which has links to other sites. Find it at www.iyhf.org

Here are a few YHA sites:
American YHA: www.hiayh.org
Australian YHA: www.yha.com.au
Dutch YHA: www.njhc.org.nl
Ireland YHA: www.irelandyha.org
New Zealand YHA: www.yha.com.nz
South Africa YHA: www.hisa.org.sa
UK YHA: www.yha.com.uk

PRIVATE BACKPACKER ESTABLISHMENTS
Private backpacker establishments are springing up all over the world. They vary greatly in their quality and services. Many can be booked from airports or directly through their advertisements in backpacker magazines.

I have found that the cheaper the room rate, the more people in the room. Some places can have up to 24 in one dorm, though many offer singles, doubles and twins.

Many of the private backpacker hostels belong to organisations. When you join the organisation, you usually receive discounts on accommodation and other travel-related services. The following are some private hostel organisations that I have discovered via the Internet:

Worldwide
VIP Backpacker Resorts have listings of some 130 hostels in Australia, 70 in New Zealand and 500 around the world. Website address: www.backpackers.com.au/welcome.html
Europe: www.hostelseurope.com/welcome.html
Australia, New Zealand and Thailand
Nomads Hostels Australia: www.nomads-backpackers.com
New Zealand only
Budget Backpacker Hostels (BBH) have over 200 hostels on both the North and South Islands listed. There is a convenient location map. Website address: www.backpacker.co.nz

For budget accommodation, you may also like to try **YMCAs** and **YWCAs**. Website addresses: www.ymca.com *or* www.ywca.com

B&B accommodation

B&Bs (bed and breakfasts) are synonymous with accommodation in the UK. Check out the website below where over 300 B&Bs are listed. There are also pictures of individual properties. Website address: www.beduk.co.uk

For B&Bs in the USA try www.bedandbreakfastusa.com

Camping grounds

Camping grounds are found worldwide. They have areas set aside for travellers with their own tents and there are powered sites for those with campervans, etc. There are usually on-site vans and cabins available for nightly and weekly hire. Keep in mind that in some areas, such as Europe, you may need to pay for a hot shower. Therefore, before you take all your clothes off and turn the hot water on, make sure you don't need to have change handy for the meter.

Motoring organisations usually have booklets listing camping grounds. You may need to be a member of the organisation to obtain them for free. Make sure you obtain the appropriate permits to enter some areas, e.g. Aboriginal or Native American Indian lands.

College campuses

During term breaks, colleges often have accommodation available. For details, contact the colleges directly. Tourist authorities may be able to provide contact details. A number of campuses have websites.

Hotel chains

Whether you are travelling on a tight budget or have plenty of money to spend, there are many international and national hotel chains offering accommodation. Contact them directly for their listings or see your nearest travel agent.

Holiday apartments

Holiday apartments are excellent if you are spending a week or two in the one place. They are usually self-contained with cooking facilities which will save on the expense of eating meals out all the time. This type of accommodation can be a little expensive but is popular in major tourist centres such as the Gold Coast, Australia; Miami, Florida; the Balearic Islands and Costa del Sol, Spain.

LONG-TERM ACCOMMODATION

While there is an abundance of short-term accommodation available around the world, finding somewhere long-term to live can prove to be the hardest thing you will have to do while overseas. This is why, as you will discover, many travellers live in hostels long-term.

There are other options available, including bedsits and studios. If you have never heard of a bedsit before don't worry, many haven't. A bedsit is basically a house rolled into one little room. Therefore in this room (which will vary in size) you will find a bed (either single, twin or double), a wardrobe, a television, a small fridge and cooking facilities. Sometimes bedsits will have a small kitchen and/or a bathroom but usually, you will share a bathroom with other bedsit occupants. These bedsits are always clustered together in one house. They will have different names in different parts of the world, but basically offer the same type of accommodation. A studio is similar to a bedsit but usually has a kitchen and bathroom.

Flat and house sharing

Travellers who decide to stay in one place for a while usually look to get into a furnished flat or house share.

If you have never been in a flat- or house-share situation before, establish before you move in: How often is the rent paid and to whom? Is there a deposit/bond/key money to be paid and who is it paid to? Does it go to an official body for safe keeping, does the landlord receive it or does it go to the outgoing traveller? How much are the bills and how are they worked out? Do you buy your own food or is there a central kitty which everyone contributes to? Do you cook your own food or prepare meals together? Are there particular times for the bathroom? How much hot water is available—enough for everyone to have a shower or bath in the morning? Is there a roster for chores or will everyone do their own share of the housework? What is the policy on friends staying?

If you do decide to put your name on a lease, consider that you will need to give the landlord/agent one month's rent in advance along with one month's deposit/bond/key money before you can move in.

If the place is furnished, go through a contents inventory with the landlord/agent to make sure that everything listed on the inventory actually exists. Do point out any pre-existing damage to the furniture, any stains on the carpet, if cutlery is missing, etc., and make sure these things are recorded on the inventory. This way, you cannot be accused of creating the damage and made to either pay for it, or have a percentage of your deposit/bond/key money taken to cover the repair, the cleaning or the replacement of the item. If you move into an unfurnished place, you can always sell the furniture you have bought to an incoming traveller before you leave.

When you put your name on a lease you will most likely need to have the gas, electricity, water and telephone connected. You may be required to pay a deposit for these services. This deposit will be refunded when you advise the authority to close the account, or it may be used as part (or full) payment of your first bill.

Many travellers have a pay phone connected—that way you pay for calls as you go. This also stops people making long-distance phone calls then leaving without paying their share of the bill.

Do advise the appropriate water, gas, electricity and phone authorities that you have moved in and you require the name on the address changed. This way, you will only pay for usage from the date you advised the authority of the change and not be liable to pay for the previous occupant's usage.

If you accumulate expensive souvenirs and furniture during your travels, you may wish to take out 'possessions' or 'contents' insurance from a local insurer.

If you have heard stories of 10 people living in a three-bedroom flat, well, they are true! There are advantages and disadvantages to such living. The biggest plus is that it's cheap. Also, after a hard day at work it is often nice to come home to talk to someone.

Unfortunately, as with all forms of sharing, living with so many people can cause personality clashes. There can also be casual relationships. You probably won't have much time to yourself either. There will also be people who don't pitch in and do their share of the housework and those who skip town without paying their share of the bills.

Before you move into any accommodation, do establish what services are nearby. Is public transport close? You don't want to walk long distances every day to reach it, particularly late at night if you do shift work. What about a supermarket? With no vehicle you will have to carry heavy shopping bags. Is there a washing machine in your accommodation? If not, where is the nearest laundrette?

Most find long-term accommodation through advertisements in newspapers, backpacker magazines and noticeboards at travel clubs. Single travellers also meet other single travellers in hostels and decide to establish a flat or house share together.

Live-in positions

If you are able to secure a live-in position, you will take care of finding both employment and accommodation in the one hit.

Popular live-in jobs include: caring for children or elderly people; bartending, particularly in the UK; domestic (housekeeper, butler, chambermaid) positions in private households or large establishments; and employment at hostels.

CHAPTER 4
Travel

It should be noted that tour operators mentioned in this chapter are listed in alphabetical order and not in any order of preference. Website addresses of tour operators have been included. Most of these sites offer you the opportunity to book and pay for your travel over the Internet. Before you do, it is your responsibility to confirm the website is secure. If you are unsure, book and pay via a travel agent, by post or in person to the tour company's head office.

SHOULD YOU PRE-PURCHASE YOUR TRAVEL?

If you walked into a travel agent this very minute and asked whether you should purchase your travel before you go, the consultant would certainly advise you to book and pay for as much as possible (preferably with them). This is because they receive a hefty commission if you do! There are pros and cons to pre-purchasing your travel.

Pre-purchase pros

- If you are travelling for a limited time only and know exactly what you want to do, then it is advisable to pre-book travel.
- Some travellers prefer to book and pay for as much as possible before they leave so they know where they stand financially. They then only need to budget for personal expenses.
- There are travel options which do need to be booked before you leave home, e.g. the BritRail, JapanRail and Eurail passes.
- If travelling during peak periods it is best to book well ahead.
- Do note that most of the major tour companies operate in many countries, so you will be able to book and pay for tours at your overseas destination. The big difference will be that you will pay for the tour in the local currency. It will be hard to know whether the tour will prove to be more expensive or cheaper than paying for it before you leave home; it all depends on the exchange rate at the time. Losing out on this

exchange rate and having to pay more for the tour overseas than what you would have at home doesn't matter to some, as it can be minimal. If it matters to you, you could always contact home and have someone there book and pay for the trip.

Pre-purchase cons

- If you pre-book and your plans change, you are stuck with your booking. There are hefty cancellation fees if you no longer wish (without a serious reason) to go on the tour.
- There are many small tour operators you don't normally know about until you arrive in another country. I have included a number of these in this chapter. These tours can be just as good, or even better than your 'limited' choice at home.
- For more information on available travel options, refer to the 'Country/area travel options' section starting on page 49.
- When organising your travel, take into consideration working holiday visa requirements; e.g. the UK working holiday visa is for two years. At one time, if you travelled outside of the UK during these two years, the time you spent out of the country was added to your two years. This is not the case anymore. You are given two years and that is it, so organise your travel either before or after the two years to gain maximum time in the UK. This also applies to other working holiday schemes.

TRAVEL OPTIONS

Firstly, purchase your travel from agencies and airlines belonging to official bodies, for example AFTA (Australian Federation of Travel Agents) and ABTA (Association of British Travel agents), ASTA (American Society of Travel Agents), IATA (International Air Transport Association), CAAC (Civil Aviation Administration of China), etc. Agencies which belong to such organisations are bound by a code of ethics. You will have more recourse in receiving a refund of money if they go into liquidation or if a tour or flight is cancelled.

Air

The quickest way to travel from A to B is to fly. Depending on the route chosen, your flight can include a few ice-filled drinks, wrestles with packets of peanuts, a dinner, a light refreshment, a breakfast, hopefully a snooze, a couple of trips to the loo, and a movie or two.

Cheap flights are not always the bargain they may seem to be. Such flights usually have restrictions. For example, if you are travelling long-haul, there may be five stops and a change of planes before you reach your destination. Or your airline may not have daily services, in which case you will have to fit your plans around their schedules. Or once you have booked and paid for your fare there is no changing the date you can fly, or you may have to pay to do so. If you don't mind these restrictions, then go with that airline.

Some airline tickets are cheaper at certain times of the year. Investigate prices during peak, off-peak and shoulder seasons. You may want to avoid travelling at peak times such as school holidays and long weekends. Apart from one-way and return tickets there are open jaw tickets and round-the-world air tickets. You can also purchase air passes to travel around specific countries.

One-way tickets are great if you do not know when you will be returning. Purchasing a return ticket may seem better value than a one-way ticket but the return portion is only valid for use for one year from the departure date. If you decide to stay away longer than one year, you will most likely not receive much of a ticket refund from the airline. (Though illegal, some travellers have been known to sell the return portion of their airline ticket to fellow travellers.)

Open jaw tickets allow you the freedom to fly into one city and out of another. Thus, you will have the option to use other means of transport between the two cities.

Round-the-world air tickets allow you to make a number of stops along your chosen route as long as you continue in the one direction. So do shop around to find a ticket that suits you.

If you have limited time in a destination or don't want to spend hours on a coach or train, you may consider purchasing an air pass. With one of these you can fly to major cities and organise any short tours from there, then hop on the plane to another major city. These passes are available in most countries, so speak to your travel agent.

Before you choose your airline, you might want to check baggage allowances. Most airlines allow you 20 kg of luggage, while some (depending on the route) allow two pieces of luggage. If you are tall, you may wish to find out the distance between seats as some airlines give you a few centimetres more leg room.

It is advised that you re-confirm all flights at least 72 hours before the flight. All airlines overbook flights to cover for 'no shows'. If you arrive at the airline counter and find you don't have a seat, the airline is obliged to offer you a seat on an alternative flight, or offer you free accommodation and meals until a seat is available.

Many airlines now allocate you a seat at the time of booking and not at your time of check-in. If you have a special request, such as you wish to have a window or aisle seat, mention this when you book. Also mention any special meal requirements (e.g. vegetarian or kosher) at your time of booking.

COURIER FLIGHTS

Some international courier companies offer discounted air tickets to people who act as air couriers for them. I had heard about courier travel but was a little sceptical in case I was given something illegal to carry. Reassurance from friends and the fact that the airfare was dirt-cheap meant I left my scepticism at home. The air courier company I rang was very helpful and sent me a listing of current destinations together with prices and the flying dates available. Los Angeles was available on the date I wanted to travel. I then booked and paid for my ticket like anybody else would through a travel agent.

On the day of my departure from Heathrow I was a little nervous. I followed the instructions 'to the T' and checked in a little early at the designated counter. Here they weighed my suitcase to make sure I hadn't gone over the 20 kg allowance. They also checked my confirmation documents and passport, and after a few moments the representative asked me to take a seat. Sitting with me were three other couriers. We were all going to different destinations because they only allow one courier per flight per day. So if you are travelling with a friend you will have to go on separate flights.

About 20 minutes later the representative came rushing through the check-in area with my assigned envelope. It had only just been delivered to the airport. One of the other couriers didn't have a package to carry, but that is how it goes sometimes.

I was given my plane ticket, boarding pass and instructions for arrival and departure. I boarded my British Airways flight. Yes, couriers fly on some of the best-known airlines in the world. I carried the A4 envelope of printed matter with me on board the plane and put it under the seat in front of me where it remained for the entire journey. No one asked to see it or felt threatened by it. I was treated like any other passenger, received all my meals and watched the movies. I wish I had realised it was this easy many, many flights ago.

On arrival in Los Angeles I gave the envelope to the representative who was waiting outside the aircraft's door. She took the envelope and that was it. I then proceeded through Immigration and Customs just like everybody else.

On my return journey, the procedure was the same, bar one thing. I had to carry the documents through Customs at Heathrow, then once in the arrival lounge I dialled a number (which made me feel like 007 reporting in) which told the representatives I had arrived. It was only a 10-minute wait for a representative to collect the package from me after which time I was free to go home.

As you see, it is easy acting as an air courier. There are restrictions, however: most tickets are round-trip; there is one courier per flight; there is a time limit on your length of stay; and sometimes you are allowed carry-on luggage only. Courier flights originate from several major cities around the world. The companies offering these flights usually advertise in major newspapers. You could contact major courier companies (such as DHL, Federal Express and TNT) in your city to see if they offer such flights, or you could join the **International Association of Air Travel Couriers (IAATC):**

United Kingdom address	USA address
www.aircourier.co.uk	www.courier.org
1 Kings Road	PO Box 1349
Dorchester	Lake Worth, FL 33460
Dorset DT1 1NJ	Tel: (0561) 582 8320
Tel: (01305) 264 564	Fax: (0561) 582 1581
Fax: (01305) 264 710	

As a member you will receive the bi-monthly *Air Courier Bulletin* magazine. You can also subscribe to *The Shoestring Traveler*, a bi-monthly newsletter providing first-hand courier experiences, tips and bargains for prospective air couriers. You can check both countries' IAATC websites for daily air-courier updates.

Land

WALKING AND LOCAL TRANSPORT

Personally, I think the best way to immerse yourself in another culture is to walk and explore. Sometimes, though, time does not permit this. Some places have tour guides for hire who will show you the many fascinating features of the city. Other places have walking tours available, such as London's 'Jack the Ripper' tour or Melbourne's 'Oldest Pub Crawl', or you could just study a map and get walking yourself. Do wear comfortable, broken-in shoes.

You may wish to incorporate local transport, such as the Tube, Metro, tram, taxi cab, felucca, camel, elephant or rick-shaw, into your day. Public transport is the cheapest and (usually) most efficient form of transport to get you around and allows you to get a more genuine experience of the city.

Public transport is usually divided into zones. A variety of travel tickets are available which will allow you to travel through a certain number of zones for a specific period. This period can vary from a few hours to a day to a week to a month or longer. You should check if the local transport system closes down over night. If it does, find out what alternatives are available.

Do not forget to take the name and address of your accommodation with you when you go out just in case you get lost. You can find out about local transport from tourist authorities before you go.

HITCHING

Although not recommended, many travellers do hitch because it is a cheap way to travel and you can also meet some very interesting people along the way. I had the excellent experience of being picked up by two deer hunters in the Scottish Highlands and sharing the back of their Range Rover (with two dead deer). Such people can be full of information on accommodation and work opportunities, as were my deer-hunter friends who told me staff were required at the public house where they were about to deliver the deer.

Many hitchers just stand on the side of the road and stick their thumb out, but some find it useful to have a sign with their destination written in large letters on it. It can be worthwhile calling into popular truck stops like diners and pubs, speaking to the truck drivers and seeing if any of them will give you a lift. After all, they may like some company.

Do be extremely careful about who you accept a lift from. There are many horror stories around; I won't go into any, but will say, if you don't like the look of the person offering you a lift, then don't be afraid to say 'no', you have changed your mind about accepting the lift. Or if you have accepted a lift and feel uneasy with the person, do not hesitate to ask them to stop the vehicle because you want to get out. I suggest that, if possible, females should hitch in pairs or with a male travel companion. It would also be wise to let someone (the hostel, a friend) know where you are going and your planned time of arrival, so if you do not arrive they can alert the authorities. Don't forget to advise them if your plans change.

LOCAL DAY TOURS

Day tours can easily be organised on your arrival. Many cities have coach companies offering tours which you can book from where you are staying. They will pick you up at your accommodation, take you to all the sights and provide you with a commentary, then drop you back at your lodgings at the end of the day.

Or you can take the hop-on, hop-off sightseeing buses which let you jump on and off at major sights. As the buses do 'the circuit' regularly, you can spend as much time as you like at different sights. When you've seen enough of one sight, you catch a bus to the next.

GROUP TRAVEL VERSUS GOING IT ALONE

As with everything, there are pros and cons associated when weighing up which form of travel to undertake.

Group travel pros
- Transport, accommodation, most meals and some entrance fees are included in the cost, so you only need spending money.
- There is less stress because you don't have to organise the above (which can cause fights with travel partners).
- Group travel gives you the opportunity to meet other like-minded, single travellers. You can make lasting friendships and even meet the partner of your dreams.
- Many tour companies do not charge single supplements to people travelling on their own.
- Group tours take you to the places you want to see.
- Every tour has a tour leader to assist with any problems, plus provide a rundown on the places you are visiting.
- You do not usually have to carry your luggage around, or at least not very far.
- There can be safety travelling in numbers.

Group travel cons
- There is restricted time in each place, thus only providing an overview of each place you visit, which limits you from immersing yourself in the local culture.
- No deviations are allowed to the touring schedule.
- You may get stuck with dickheads! (If you don't like a tour, you are not obliged to stay on it, but, if you leave of your own accord, you will not receive a refund for the remaining portion of the trip which you did not undertake.)

Going it alone pros
- You get the freedom to do as you please and go where you want, when you want.
- You can stay as long as you want.
- You're able to immerse yourself in the local culture.

Going it alone cons
- You must carry your luggage around.
- You spend time looking for accommodation (if you haven't pre-booked) and for places to eat, which can be frustrating.
- You may get lost looking for sights (but isn't that half the fun?). There are many companies offering group travel tours. Some

offer tours in several countries. Some use large coaches while others use mini buses so they can get 'off the beaten track'. Some are also known as jo-jos (jump-on, jump-off). This is where you can jump off at a sight, stay a couple of days, then jump on the next bus to your next destination. More information on jo-jos following.

Other coach companies specialise in a specific area or cater for a specific age group. There are also specialised tours like African safaris; trekking in Nepal; surfing safaris; eco-travel; Antarctic exploration; whale-watching; festivals like Oktoberfest; pilgrimages to the Holy City or the battlefields of Europe; sporting tours for cricket, tennis or golf; visiting Aztec or Mayan sites, or walking the Inca Trail; literary tours to Ireland to follow in James Joyce's footsteps; cultural tours—the list is endless. Some of these tours are mentioned in the 'Country/area travel options' section on page 49.

Pop into a travel agent to obtain travel brochures. Do visit a few different travel agents as some are aligned with specific tour companies and so will only give you their particular brochures. Also visit national tourist bureaus, look in the travel sections of newspapers, read travel magazines and surf the Net.

Some large tour companies include the following:

Contiki specialises in tours for 18- to 35-year-olds in Australia, Canada, New Zealand, the UK, Europe, Ireland, Africa and the USA. Website address: www.contiki.com

Encounter Overland specialises in adventure holidays and overland journeys in Asia, Africa and Central and South America. Website address: www.encounter-overland.com

Globus and Cosmos offers tours around Australia and New Zealand, the UK and Europe, Asia, Central and South America, the USA and Canada as well as some parts of Africa (Egypt, Morocco, Zimbabwe, Kenya, Tanzania and South Africa). Website address: www.globusandcosmos.com

Insight offers open-age tours and tours for 18- to 38-year-olds in Australia, the UK and Europe, eastern Mediterranean, Canada and the USA and South Africa. Website address: www.insighttours.com

Intrepid Travel offers small-group adventure travel in South-East Asia, China, Japan and India. Website address: www.intrepidtravel.com.au

Kumuka offers overland adventure tours in Africa, Latin America, the Middle East and Europe. Website address: www.kumuka.co.uk

Peregrine Adventure Travel and **Dragoman Adventure Travel** are part of the same stable, offering small-group adventure travel in Africa, Asia, India, Himalayas, Central and South America and Antarctica. Website addresses: www.peregrine.net.au or www.dragoman.co.uk

Top Deck Travel specialises in 18 to 30-something tours in Europe, Egypt, Jordan, Israel, Morocco and Turkey. They also offer an overland trip between London and Kathmandu and ski trips in Europe, Canada and the USA. Website address: www.topdecktravel.co.uk

Trafalgar Tours offers fully escorted tours in luxury coaches for open-age and 21- to 35-year-olds in Europe, the UK, eastern Mediterranean, northern Africa, the USA, Canada, Australia, New Zealand and the Orient. Website address: www.trafalgartours.com

World Expeditions offers adventure travel holidays. To quote their website they offer 'off-the-beaten-track adventures to the world's most spectacular wilderness destinations', including Australia, Central and South-East Asia, countries on the Asian subcontinent, South America and African nations. Website address: www.worldexpeditions.com.au

JO-JOS AND BACKPACKER TOURS

Jo-jos are aimed at independent travellers and backpackers and offer a more independent style of travel than a tour, but don't leave you to your own devices as when travelling on a coach or train pass. What they do is allow you to jump on and jump off, or hop on and hop off, or get on and get off, at certain points along a predetermined route. So you can get off the bus, stay a few days in a particular place and book a seat on the next bus travelling the route.

Jo-jo companies only provide the transport, so you will need to pay for accommodation. Don't worry about having to find this each night, as many jo-jos offer a hostel door-to-door service and can ring ahead to book you a bed for that night. They can also offer you suggestions on alternative accommodation if you don't wish to stay at a hostel, and will usually drop you off at that accommodation.

There are many jo-jos becoming available in a number of countries. For an overview on each, along with their contact details, refer to them under the specific country/area travel options following. They currently include:

- Africa: Baz Bus, Truck About
- Australia: Oz Experience, Wayward Bus
- Canada: Canabus, Further Still, Moose Run Adventure Tours, Moose Travel Company
- Central America: Green Tortoise Adventure Travel
- New Zealand: Kiwi Experience, Magic Bus
- Turkey: Fez Bus
- UK & Ireland: Haggis Backpackers, Hairy Hog, MacBackpackers, Outback UK, Stray Travel Network, Tir na nOg Tours
- USA: Green Tortoise Adventure Travel

COACH AND TRAIN PASSES

There are a number of coach and train passes available in a variety of countries.

Some people prefer train travel over coach travel as trains allow you to get up and walk around during your journey. They also offer sleepers and usually have meal carriages.

You will need to pick up the brochures and have a look at exactly what is on offer. Most of these passes entitle you either to unlimited travel within a specified timeframe (e.g. unlimited travel for 15 days) or to a certain number of days' travel within a certain period (e.g. you are allowed 10 days' travel in 30 days).

The travel time on your pass begins the day you first present it to be used. A number of publications on train travel, including timetables, have been published. Look for them in book stores.

Countries which have the infrastructure to offer train and/or coach passes include: South Africa, Australia, Canada, China, Europe, India, Japan, New Zealand, the United Kingdom and the Republic of Ireland and the United States of America.

Details on individual passes are to be found in the 'Country/area travel options' section following.

CARS, VANS AND OTHER VEHICLES

Flexibility is the name of the game when you travel in your own vehicle. You can go where you want (including out-of-the-way places that coach and train travellers often miss), when you want.

Keep the following things in mind when considering driving overseas: what side of the road to drive on (most southern hemisphere countries drive on the left, while northern hemisphere countries, bar the UK and the Republic of Ireland, drive on the right); the different road signs, speed limits, drink-driving limits and other regulations.

There are various ways to get your hands on the wheel of a car. You could hire, relocate, share a lift or buy a vehicle.

HIRING VEHICLES

At some time during your travels you may hire a vehicle. Make sure the rate you are quoted has no hidden charges, such as stamp duty, which may be added after you have agreed to hire the car. Ensure there is roadside service in case of a breakdown. Check if the vehicle will have unlimited kilometres/miles, or whether you have to pay a certain rate for each kilometre/mile travelled. Find out about insurance and whether there is an excess to pay if you have an accident. What if you do have an accident—what is the procedure?

You can hire vehicles before you go travelling. Some airlines are aligned with car rental companies and offer special rates for those travelling with them. You can book through travel agents or else hire a vehicle on your arrival directly from car rental companies at the airport. It is worth noting that the price in renting an automatic car compared to a manual car can vary greatly in different countries. For example, in the UK, most people drive manual cars, so it is far cheaper to rent one of these. But in the USA, most people drive automatic cars, and you will be hard pressed to find a manual car, so it is cheaper to rent an automatic. Some companies may require the driver to be 21 years old or over, or even 25 years and over.

You don't necessarily have to return the car to where you hired it, as one-way rentals are available. This is also known as relocating.

BUYING/SELLING A VEHICLE
Buying a vehicle is an option many travellers choose. One drawback is the up-front cost required to purchase the vehicle, but you will be selling it at the end of your journey anyway. It is wise, and cheaper, if there are a few of you who can pool your resources, to buy a vehicle together.

Even though price is a major concern, what you really need is a guarantee that the vehicle you purchase will complete the travelling you want to do without needing major repairs shortly after purchase or during your travels. Therefore, make sure you have someone mechanically-minded to give your chosen vehicle the 'once over'. Also ensure all the appropriate paperwork is in place, including printed information stating the car is fully roadworthy, before you hand over any money. Do purchase appropriate motor vehicle insurance. Though the vehicle may be roadworthy, it is essential to carry some tools and spare parts. It should go without saying to check the water and oil before you head off on any trip.

Some car dealers specialise in backpacker vehicles (campervans, combi vans, station wagons, etc.), which provide both transport and accommodation. These dealers often have a buy-back scheme which is discussed with you at the time of purchase. The buy-back price may be less than what you could get if you sold the vehicle privately but at the same time, you have a guaranteed buyer.

LIFT SHARING
Lift sharing is an option for travellers. There are people out there who have bought a car but don't have the bodies to fill it, so they advertise for travel companions.

Most lifts are advertised on hostel noticeboards and can read something like this: 'Person required to make up 4th on a ramble up east coast. Leaving Sydney Monday to be in Byron Bay by Friday. Contact ...', or 'Two people required to join two others in combi van leaving London mid-June for three-month trip through Europe. Contact ...' These lifts are also advertised in backpacker magazines.

CYCLING TOURS
Some countries with flat terrain are ideal for cycle tours (though I have seen people riding up steep mountains in the French Alps). The Netherlands is a prime example. For a few Dutch florin you can hire a bike for a few hours or longer. You may wish to contact your nearest cycling club where you may receive bicycle advice.

Water

Sailing the world's waterways are a huge variety of seacraft, ranging from feluccas on the Nile to a luxury liner cruising the Pacific.

Some ferry services are included in coach and rail passes, such as Scandinavian and Mediterranean ferry services with the Eurail Pass. Otherwise you can easily purchase a fare near the dock. Ferries vary in size and either take foot passengers or are the 'roll-on, roll-off' type on which you can take your vehicle with you.

In recent years cruise liners have had a resurgence in popularity. This has led not only to an increase in the number of vessels cruising the world but to a jump in work opportunities for travellers. See the 'Cruise-line positions' and 'Yacht crewing' sections of Chapter 7.

COUNTRY/AREA TRAVEL OPTIONS

All countries have transport available, though some have more options than others. For instance, Europe has the infrastructure for travel via plane, train, coach and other vehicles, while China is best travelled by rail.

The purpose of this country/area travel section is to provide you with information on available options. These suggestions are not exhaustive. The suggestions only provide you with a starting point, and will require further research on your part. I'm sure you will find more options as you begin your research and travels.

Please note that most air, coach and train passes are designed for overseas travellers (and not usually locals), which is why they must be purchased outside the country in which the passes are valid. In some cases, though, the passes or alternative passes can be purchased in the particular country.

Visit your nearest travel agent to pick up the brochures on the country/area you are interested in. Also contact tourist information centres for information. Either purchase a travel guide or borrow one from the library specialising in the area you wish to visit. You can also surf the Net for relevant information.

AFRICA

The African continent is extremely large and consists of over 40 countries which are very diverse. To visit all of these countries and to appreciate what each has to offer would take an extensive amount of time. Therefore, you should work out what it is you want to see and experience. Do you want to go on safari? Or do you want to see the gorillas? Or do you want an African beach-resort holiday? Once you know this you can proceed to work out the best way to do it, and when to do it.

Advice I have received about travelling Africa independently is that it is very difficult to do so. A major consideration is the ever-changing political climates which can interfere with the best-laid plans by making certain countries off limits to travellers. Other things to contend with include a lack of services, but the availability of services does depend on individual countries. For instance, Kenya, Zimbabwe and South Africa (after years of isolation due to Apartheid) are well adept for travellers and offer coach and train services. The seasons are another consideration. Would you be appropriately prepared to be in the Sahara during the hottest time of the year? What about coping at borders? In most cases you will part with 'bribe' money during negotiations with border officials at border crossings. For these reasons many undertake a tour.

If you are serious about travelling Africa independently, I highly suggest you purchase, or borrow from the library, specialist travel guides or travel literature of people's first-hand experiences of travelling Africa this way. You should find valuable information on appropriate vehicles and equipment to take, as well as information on accommodation, visas, clothing and routes.

International Bicycle Fund has a very good website for those interested in travelling Africa by bicycle (which could be used for other vehicles). Information on travelling in individual African countries is provided with a lowdown on the state of the roads and recommendations as to whether the country is conducive to bicycle riding. For instance, it advises that Egypt isn't a country suited to bicycle riding, while Kenya, is a very bicycle-friendly country. Website address: www.ibike.org

AIR

As Africa is so large, an option may be to include some flights into your itinerary. You may consider purchasing an open jaw ticket and fly into one city, travel overland, then fly out of another city. You should see your travel agent or surf the Net to see what is available through such airlines as South African Airways, Air Zimbabwe, Air Namibia, Ethiopian Airlines, etc.

TOURS

Going on an organised tour is a good way to see Africa. Tour companies offer a variety of travel options, including overland journeys which take you from one end of the continent to the other, or those which concentrate on specific countries, e.g. Kenya, Tanzania, Zimbabwe, Botswana, Namibia and South Africa. Within these, there are a few options, including a safari to a game park, visiting natural wonders such as Mount Kilimanjaro or the Victoria Falls, undertaking a 'gorilla trek', cruising by canoe on famous rivers (Zambezi), meeting the locals (like the Masai Mara people), relaxing on a beach, or undertaking a dive package in a coastal resort.

Because of the terrain, tours are undertaken in 4WD-size or specially adapted overland vehicles catering for limited passenger numbers. Accommodation varies and can include tents, hostels, huts, lodges, hotels and home stays. To find out more, pick up brochures from travel agents. Some tour companies include:

Acacia: www.acacia-africa.com
Contiki: www.contiki.com
Dragoman Adventure Travel: www.dragoman.co.uk
Encounter Overland: www.encounter-overland.com
Guerba: www.guerba.co.uk
Kumuka: www.kumuka.co.uk
Peregrine Adventure Travel: www.dragoman.co.uk
Trafalgar Tours: www.trafalgartours.com
World Expeditions: www.worldexpeditions.com.au

JO-JOS

Southern Africa has the **Baz Bus** offering a hop-on, hop-off service between Cape Town (South Africa) and Victoria Falls (Zimbabwe). You can begin your journey at either end. You can also take a route into Swaziland. Pick up information on the Baz Bus from South African Tourist bureaus and at hostels in South Africa.
Baz Bus: Tel: +27 (021) 439 2343
www.icon.co.za/~bazbus

Truck About, a British company, offers a jo-jos bus taking in Kenya, Tanzania, Malawi, Zimbabwe and Botswana. Two passes are available: *Blue Pass* taking in Kenya and Tanzania only; and *Red Pass* taking in Kenya, Tanzania, Malawi, Zambia, Zimbabwe and Botswana.
Truck About
4 Barnfield Place
London E14 9YA, UK
Tel: +44 (020) 7536 9316
Fax: +44 (020) 7515 6969

COACH PASSES
Greyhound provides coach services in South Africa. You can purchase travel passes for unlimited travel. For example, seven days, travel in 30 days. Website address: www.greyhound.co.za

TRAINS
Spoornet runs the **Main Line Passenger Service** trains and the *Blue Train* in Southern Africa. Website address: www.spoornet.co.za

Great train journeys
The Blue Train—Cape Town to Pretoria and Pretoria to Victoria Falls, and vice versa. Website address: www.bluetrain.co.za
The Rovos Rail—Cape Town to Dar es Salaam and vice versa (the most luxurious train in the world). Website address: www.rovos.co.za

BUSH TAXIS AND OTHER LOCAL TRANSPORT
Some African countries have bush taxis to take you to another city, or in some cases, another country. To find these, contact tourist information centres, ask at hotel receptions or ask the drivers directly. Some travellers pick up lifts in Africa. For instance, in Kenya, you may catch a lift in a converted pick-up truck known as a matatu.

THE ANTARCTIC

The Antarctic is a desolate and cold landmass once only accessible to explorers and researchers. If you are interested in experiencing the natural wonders and wildlife of Antarctica, there are two options available. You can go on a flight over the Antarctic or undertake a sailing trip into the area. Both trips are accompanied by guest lecturers who will discuss the area and wildlife with you. During the southern hemisphere spring and summer (October to February), Qantas offer flights over the Antarctic from Australia that usually last around 12 hours. For details try www.antarcticaflights.com.au

Tour companies offering sailing trips into the Antarctic include:
Peregrine Travel Adventures: www.peregrine.net.au
World Expeditions: www.worldexpeditions.com.au

AUSTRALIA

Australia is an extremely large country with huge distances between major centres. To fully appreciate everything Australia has to offer you would need an extensive amount of time. Fortunately, there are many forms of transport to travel Australia. You could therefore use a number of options to complete your travel. And the good news is that most of the options, apart from certain air passes, can be purchased in the country.

AIR PASSES
As well as point-to-point flights and open jaw tickets there are air passes available to non-residents with the two major Australian airlines, Ansett Australia and Qantas. Both airlines offer overseas visitors travel passes for travel by flights.

TOURS
A number of tour operators offer organised tours around Australia. Tours vary in length from short trips in specific areas to longer tours taking you from one end of the country to the other.
AAT Kings: www.aatkings.com.au
Australian Pacific: www.aptours.com.au
Connections 18–35s: www.connections1835.com.au
Contiki: www.contiki.com.au
Globus and Cosmos: www.globusandcosmos.com
Insight Tours: www.insighttours.com
Trafalgar Tours: www.trafalgartours.com
World Expeditions: www.worldexpeditions.com.au

There are also a number of independent tour operators which take you to 'out of the way' places.

One such company, **Wayward Bus**, offers tours which often take you 'off the beaten track' through south-east Australia. You can book a tour once you are in Australia at backpacker travel centres.

Fruitbowl—Sydney to Adelaide and vice versa through the fruit-growing areas. You may even pick up work along the way!

Over the Top—from Sydney to Melbourne via Canberra and vice versa along the Alpine Way through the Snowy Mountains.

Mountains and Rivers—a tour between Sydney and Melbourne.

Classic Coast—from Adelaide to Melbourne via the coast.

Wayward also offers *Face the Outback*, an overland tour from Adelaide to Alice Springs through the outback.
Wayward Bus: www.waywardbus.com.au
237 Hutt Street
Adelaide SA 5000
Tel: (08) 8232 6646
Fax: (08) 8232 1455

JO-JOS

Oz Experience provides alternative coach transport for backpackers and independent travellers. The company offers several passes which often take you 'off the beaten track'. The passes can be purchased within Australia from backpacker travel agencies and vary in length. Some passes allow you to do a circuit, by returning you to where you joined the bus, while others allow you to travel in one direction. There are a number of interestingly named passes which cover the eastern and central parts of Australia, these include: *Fair Dinkum, Strewth, Bruce, Cobber, Boomerang, Fish Hook/Goanna, Vegemight/Dunny Door, Matey, Donga* and *Big Rock*, to name a few.
Oz Experience: www.ozexperience.com
Shop 401, Kingsgate Shopping Centre
Darlinghurst Road
Kings Cross, Sydney NSW 2011
Tel: (02) 9368 1766
Fax: (02) 9368 0908

COACH PASSES

Many travellers purchase a coach pass to travel Australia. There are many passes available which are offered by two major coach lines, Greyhound Pioneer Australia and McCaffertys. Passes can be purchased in Australia from coach terminals and backpacker travel agents.

Greyhound Pioneer Australia have over 20 flexible coach passes available. They include *Aussie Explorer Passes* which allow you to stop off in unlimited destinations on a predetermined route. There are a number of passes available including *Aussie Highlights, Best of the Outback, Whitsunday Pass, Pearl Diver, Southern Sea and Sun* and *Coast to Coast*, to name a few.

Also available are *Aussie Day Passes* where you can purchase travel in lots of seven, 10, 15 or 21 days. Each trip you take equals one day of travel. You can also purchase an *Aussie Kilometre Pass* where you work out the kilometres you wish to travel then purchase a pass in 1000 km blocks. Website address: www.greyhound.com.au

McCaffertys offer two passes: *Travel Passes* offer unlimited stops along predetermined routes such as the east coast. The *Australian Roamer Pass* lets you work out the kilometres you wish to travel, then purchase the kilometres. Website address: www.mccaffertys.com.au

TRAIN PASSES
Australia's rail network is not as extensive as the coach services. Each State has a network, however the *Austrailpass* (only available to overseas visitors) allows unlimited travel for several days on all networks. There are also other train passes available, e.g. the *East Coast Discovery Pass* which allows you to travel the east coast. The *Westrail Discovery Pass* lets you experience Western Australia. Most link a great train journey (see below) with flights and bus trips.

Great train journeys
The Ghan—Sydney to Adelaide to Alice Springs and vice versa.
The Indian Pacific—Sydney to Perth via Adelaide and vice versa.
The Queenslander—Brisbane to Cairns and vice versa.

BUYING/SELLING A VEHICLE
A lot of visitors purchase vehicles from one of the backpacker dealerships advertising in *TNT Magazine Australia* and *Aussie Backpacker* magazines. Many visit the Kings Cross Car Market in Sydney. This is where travellers sell their vehicles along with camping equipment and other items. The market also offers advice on all aspects of buying and selling a vehicle including registration and insurance. Check out their website at www.carmarket.com.au

You may also like to visit the Travellers Auto Barn. Website address: www.travellers-autobarn.com.au

Be aware that these backpacker vehicles may have travelled around Australia many times.

CANADA

Canada is a large country with huge distances between major centres. To appreciate everything Canada has to offer would take a lot of time. Fortunately, there are many ways to travel Canada. You could therefore use a number of options to complete your travel.

AIR PASSES
You may like to include flights in your travel plans. There are several regional air passes available from Canadian Airlines and American airlines mentioned under the United States of America section.

TOURS AND JO-JOS

There are several tour operators offering tours around Canada. There are those which offer tours in the most visited provinces of British Columbia and Alberta on the west Ccoast and Ontario and Quebec on the east coast. Coast-to-coast tours are also available. See your nearest travel agent for brochures. Some companies include:

Contiki: **www.contiki.com**
Globus and Cosmos: **www.globusandcosmos.com**
Insight Tours: www.insighttours.com
Trafalgar Tours: www.trafalgartours.com

There are a number of smaller companies providing backpacker and jump-on, jump-off touring. These include the following:
Canabus Tours offers a seven-day, six-night journey called the *Ontario Experience*. As the name suggests, the tour specialises in the province of Ontario. It can be booked from hostels in Canada.
Canabus Tours Inc: www.canabus.com
74 Gerrard Street East
Toronto, Ontario
M5B 1G6, Canada
Tel: (0416) 977 8311
Fax: (0416) 977 9533

Further Still offers adventure tours across Canada. There are a number of tours available including *Western Tour*, *Eastern Tour*, *Coast to Coast* and *Ontario Trek*. There are also day trips available.
Further Still: **www.furtherstill.com**
4549 Cataract Avenue
Niagara Falls, Ontario
L2E 3M2, Canada
Tel: (0905) 371 8747
Fax: (0905) 357 9845

Moose Run Adventure Tours offers a 10-day *Moose Run*, departing from Vancouver and including the Rocky Mountains of British Columbia and Alberta. You can book at hostels in Vancouver.
Moose Run Adventure Tours: www.mooserun.com
1653 Coquitlam Avenue
Coquitlam, BC
V3B 1H8, Canada
Tel: (0604) 944 3007
Fax: (0604) 944 3091

Moose Travel Company offers a jump-on, jump-off bus in the provinces of Ontario and Quebec. There are three transport packages, *The Beaver Trail*, *The Loonie Trail* and *The Moose Trail*. There is also *The Niagara Trail* giving you a few days to appreciate the Niagara Falls. You can purchase your tour at major hostels in Toronto, Montreal, Ottawa and Quebec City.
Moose Travel Company: www.moosetravelco.com
499 Greig Circle
Newmarket
ON L3Y 8S7, Canada
Tel: (0905) 853 4760
Fax: (0905) 853 4761

COACH PASSES
Greyhound Canada is Canada's largest inter-city bus line, running from Vancouver in the west, to Toronto in the east, the Yukon and Northern Territories up north and south along the US border. It offers point-to-point sales plus several passes through Canada which you can buy on arrival. Website address: www.greyhound.ca

TRAIN PASSES
The **Via Rail Canada** network is Canada's train service. You can purchase a *Canrailpass* to travel on this network. The pass offers 12 days' unlimited travel in economy class during a 30-day period. Extra days of travel can be added. Website address: www.viarail.ca

Also available is the *North American Rail Pass* which allows travel in Canada on any VIA train and in the United States on Amtrak trains. Website address: www.amtrak.com

Great train journeys
The Rocky Mountaineer—Vancouver through the Rocky Mountains to Calgary and vice versa.

CENTRAL AND SOUTH AMERICA

The landmass of Central and South America is extremely large and is made up of a number of countries.
Central America: Mexico, Guatemala, Belize, Honduras, El Salvador, Nicaragua, Costa Rica and Panama.
South America: Colombia, Venezuela, Guyana, Surinam, Ecuador, Peru, Bolivia, Brazil, Paraguay, Argentina, Uruguay and Chile.

To visit all or some of these countries and to appreciate all they have to offer would take up an extensive amount of time. Therefore, you should work out what it is you want to see and experience, then work out the best way to do it.

Many travellers either spend a long time in one country or link several countries together with flights, independent travel and tours.

The vastness of Central and South America has led to individual countries having very good internal transport infrastructures. During my research for this section, unfortunately, I found that there wasn't one place I could go to for information on such transport systems. Instead, I had to visit each individual country's tourist bureaus for the information and piece it all together myself. I suggest therefore, you do the same or purchase or borrow from the library a specialist travel guide which details the travel options available.

AIR PASSES

Most countries have their own airline or a number of airlines servicing major capitals in their own country and others. There are point-to-point sales available, along with open jaw tickets which would allow you to fly into one city, travel overland, then fly out of another. If you only want to travel in one country then you may consider purchasing an air pass. Some local airlines include: Aerolineas Argentinas, Aero Mexico, Lan Chile and Varig (a Brazilian airline).

TOURS

There are a number of tour companies offering tours to Central and South American countries. Tours vary, from those which travel overland through several countries to those which specialise in one country. Some tours let you experience past cultures, e.g. walking the 'Inca Trail' into Machu Picchu. Others incorporate sailing the Amazon, trekking the Andes or partying at carnivals, such as the Carnivale in Rio de Janeiro. Some specialist tour companies include:

Dragoman Adventure Travel: www.dragoman.co.uk
Encounter Overland: www.encounter-overland.com
Globus and Cosmos: www.globusandcosmos.com
Peregrine Adventure Travel: www.peregrine.net.au
World Expeditions: www.worldexpeditions.com.au

Green Tortoise Adventure Travel offers 'stretch-out-and-sleep-while-we-drive' tours. Basically, by day, the coach acts as a normal coach tour taking you to places and allowing you to do things you want to do. By night, the seats turn into bunk beds.

Tours are available in North and Central America. They can be purchased at their main office which operates at the Green Tortoise

hostel in San Francisco and the Green Tortoise hostel in Seattle.
Green Tortoise Adventure Travel: www.greentortoise.com
494 Broadway
San Francisco
CA 94133, USA
Tel: (0415) 834 1000

BUSES
Buses are a principle means of transport in Central and South America so most countries have their own bus operations which are well developed. Most towns have a central bus terminal where you can purchase a ticket from one of the local bus companies.

The state of the roads varies from country to country. Most have very good sealed roads while others have unsealed roads which can resemble dry creek beds.

Like the roads, the quality of the buses can vary from old American school buses to luxurious coaches. If bus travel is your chosen form of transport, be prepared to share your passage with farm animals and locals carrying produce. Also be prepared for rough rides and hairy journeys around cliff bends.

SEA PASSAGES
There is the possibility of travelling to the coastal regions of some Central and South American countries by catching a ride on a yacht or working your way on a freighter. A popular area to catch a lift is from either end of the Panama Canal or from the Caribbean.

If you wish to sail along the Amazon River, there are cargo and other sea vessels available.

EGYPT AND ISRAEL

Although Egypt is on the African continent and Israel is part of the Middle East, these two countries are often visited together. Due to the large numbers of visitors to these countries it is easy to undertake independent travel. You can organise day tours from your accommodation once you have arrived.

TOURS
Most of the tour companies who offer tours through Africa and Europe offer tours to Egypt and Israel. So if you want to cruise the Nile in a felucca, or explore the Pyramids, there is a tour for you.
Acacia: www.acacia-africa.com
Contiki: www.contiki.com.au

Dragoman: www.dragoman.co.uk
Encounter Overland: www.encounter-overland.com
Globus and Cosmos: www.globusandcosmos.com
Insight Tours: www.insighttours.com
Peregrine Adventure Travel: www.peregrine.net.au
Top Deck: www.topdeck.co.uk
Trafalgar Tours: www.trafalgartours.com

EUROPE, SCANDINAVIA AND THE COMMONWEALTH OF INDEPENDENT STATES

For the purposes of this section, countries in Western, Central and Eastern Europe, Scandinavia and the Commonwealth of Independent States have been grouped together. This is because a lot of the travelling options in these regions are linked.

AIR PASSES

If you have limited time you may wish to include flights in your travel plans. This could allow you to fly into major centres where you can then undertake day or extended tours. You could also fly into one city, travel overland, then fly out of another city.

Europe, Scandinavia and the Commonwealth of Independent States are serviced by many airlines including national and charter companies, e.g. Alitalia, Air France, Finnair, KLM, Lauda Air, Olympic Airlines, SAS (Scandinavian Airways), Swissair, etc. You may wish to contact them to find out about air passes and open jaw tickets.

TOURS

There are many companies offering tours of Europe, Scandinavia and the CIS. Some market coach tours specifically for the 18 to 30-something age group. Tours range in length from weeks to a few months. Accommodation options include camping, hotels and the chance to stay in traditional accommodation such as a *gasthof* in Austria, a chateau in France, a villa in Italy or a chalet in Switzerland.

Most of these tour companies offer special ski packages and special trips to festivals such as the Running of the Bulls in Pamplona, Spain, the Oktoberfest in Munich, Germany and Hogmonay in Scotland. Tour companies include:

Contiki: www.contiki.com
Globus and Cosmos: www.globusandcosmos.com
Insight Tours: www.insighttours.com.au
Top Deck: www.topdeck.co.uk
Trafalgar Tours: www.trafalgartours.com

JO-JOS
Busabout provides a flexible coach service through Europe. There are two ways you can travel with them, either purchase a set itinerary or a hop-on, hop-off pass. Website address: www.busabout.com.uk

There are two set itineraries available:

The 16-day *Northern Exposure*; which visits France, the Netherlands, Germany, the Czech Republic and Austria; and

The 20-day *Southern Stroll*; which visits France, Switzerland, Germany and Italy.

There are two hop-on, hop-off passes available:

Consecutive Pass, which allows unlimited travel within the entire network. There are five of these available ranging from 15 days to a five-month season pass.

Flexi-pass allows you to choose the number of travelling days you want within a set timeframe, e.g. seven days in one month.

For those visiting Turkey, you might consider the independent tour company **Fez Bus** which offers a number of hop-on, hop-off passes including *Turkish Delight* (a circuit around Turkey), *Beach Bum* (for those who just want to sit on the beach), *Cave Dweller*, *Trooper* (which visits Gallipoli), *Eruption* and *Silk Road* (for those coming from Greece). You can purchase a pass in Turkey at the main office.

Fez Bus: www.feztravel.com
Akbiyik Caddesi No. 15
Sultanahmet, Istanbul, Turkey
Tel: (0212) 516 9024
Fax: (0212) 518 5085

COACH PASSES
Eurolines is the European arm of the United Kingdom's National Express coach network. Eurolines provide coach travel between 48 cities around Europe. As well as point-to-point tickets you can purchase a *Eurolines Pass* offering 30 or 60 days of unlimited travel.

You can purchase your pass once overseas. As many Australians begin their European journey in London, you can buy a pass at the London Coach Station, Buckingham Palace Road, London (near the Victoria Train Station). Or see Eurolines or National Express' websites. Website addresses: www.eurolines.co.uk *or* www.nationalexpress.co.uk

TRAIN PASSES
Various rail passes give you the opportunity for extensive travel throughout Europe or within specific countries. The **Eurail Pass** is

synonymous with travel through Europe. There are also individual country rail passes including French Rail Pass, German Rail Pass, Austria Rail Pass, Scan Rail Pass, Balkans Rail Pass, Swiss Rail Pass, Benelux Tour Rail Pass and the Spanish Flexipass.

If you did not purchase a Eurail Pass before you left home, you can purchase an Inter-Rail Pass (details following).

Information on the Eurail Pass can be accessed via the BritRail site at: www.britrail.co.uk

If you have been resident in the UK or Europe for six months or more, consider the **Inter-Rail Pass**, allowing train travel in 28 European countries. Passes are available in eight different geographical zones. You can purchase a pass to travel in any one zone for 22 days or add a number of them together for one month of travel.

As many begin their European jaunts from London you can purchase an Inter-Rail Pass from the International Ticket Sales Desk at Victoria Train Station in London or have a look at their website. Website address: www.inter-rail.co.uk

You may also like to look at the Rail Europe website at: www.raileurope.co.uk

If railing Europe is your choice of travel, then you may consider purchasing a timetable. A number of books listing train timetables are available.

Great train journeys
Orient Express—There are several routes including:
Venice to London via Paris and vice versa;
Venice to Rome and vice versa;
Venice to London via Prague and Paris, London;
Venice to London via Lucerne and Paris; and
Paris to Istanbul via Budapest and Bucharest.
Website address: www.orient-expresstrains.com
The Glacier Express—St Moritz to Zermatt, Switzerland, and vice versa.

SEA CRAFT
There are a number of ferries and hovercrafts servicing Europe. Many passages are included in rail and coach passes.

There are those which link the UK with Ireland and the UK with the continent. There are ferries servicing the Mediterranean, particularly the Greek Islands and ferries linking the Scandinavian countries with Europe and the Commonwealth of Independent States.

Most ferries take 'foot passengers' and offer a 'roll-on, roll-off' service for those with vehicles.

Irish Ferries (between Ireland and Europe): www.irishferries.ie
Stena Sealink Ferries (between the UK, Ireland and the Netherlands): www.stenaline.com
Scandinavian Seaways (DFDS) (between Denmark, Sweden and Germany): www.scansea.com
Royal Olympic Cruises (around the Mediterranean): www.royalolympiccruises.com

INDIAN SUBCONTINENT

For the purposes of this section, countries include: Bangladesh, Bhutan, India, Pakistan, Nepal and Sri Lanka.

These countries are diverse. To visit all of them and to appreciate what each has to offer would demand a great deal of time. Therefore, you should work out what it is you want to see and experience. Then, work out the best way to do it and, when to do it.

AIR PASSES
You may wish to include flights in your itinerary. Several local airlines offer flights including: Indian Airlines, Royal Nepal Airlines, etc.

TOURS
Many people who visit this area undertake a tour. Trekking tours of the Himalayas are particularly popular. Tours are available at differing grades for people at various fitness levels including gentle (which doesn't require strenuous activity), moderate (for any reasonably fit person who can walk up to six hours a day) and adventurous. The trekking season is from late spring to summer (September to May). Trekking can be undertaken independently and organised once over there, as major cities including Delhi, Khathmandu, etc., offer outfitters, Sherpas who offer their services as tour guides, trekking tours, etc. Some specialist tour companies include:
Encounter Overland: www.encounter-overland.com
Intrepid Travel: www.intrepidtravel.com.au
World Expeditions: www.worldexpeditions.com.au

TRAIN PASSES
India—Trains are a principle form of transport in India. It is said that some 10 million Indians travel by train every day. The India Rail system is said to be the second largest rail system in the world with around 65,000 km of track which visit some 7,000 stations.

India Rail offers the *Indrail Pass* for overseas visitors. Pass holders are entitled to unlimited travel for the length of their pass. Passes are available for ½, 1, 2, 4, 7, 15, 21, 30, 60 and 90 days of travel. See a travel agent or Indian Tourist Board office for details.

Great train journeys
Palace on Wheels—From Delhi, through parts of India and looping back to Delhi.

JAPAN

Japan is made up of several islands; all are well serviced by air, ferry, coach and train services. Depending on your available time, you may consider linking a number of options to complete your travels.

AIR PASSES
Japan is serviced by three airlines; All Nippon Airways (ANA), Japan Airlines (JAL) and Japan Air System (JAS). Ask them about air passes.

TOURS
There are a number of tour companies offering tours through Japan. See your travel agent for details.

TRAINS AND TRAIN PASSES
Japan has a well-developed rail system offering a great array of travel options. **Japan Rail (JR)** is a group of six companies covering the entire country. *Shinkansen*, or bullet trains, are synonymous with rail travel in Japan. The whole system is noted for running on time and for trains stopping at platforms with pinpoint accuracy.

The cheapest way to travel Japan is to purchase a *Japan Rail Pass*. These are available for consecutive seven, 14 and 21 days of travel. There are two types: the *Green Pass* for travel in the superior-class Green cars, and the *Ordinary Pass*. Passes may be used on affiliated buses and ferries. Passes must be purchased outside Japan and are only available to tourists for sightseeing. Travellers with working holiday visas are not entitled to purchase a Japan Rail Pass.

COACH AND FERRY
The JR train system also operates intra-city buses while other private lines follow expressways to major cities. You can use your Japan Rail Pass on affiliated coach services and ferry services.

NEW ZEALAND

New Zealand is made up of two major islands, the North Island and the South Island. Both have travel networks available.

AIR PASSES
If your time is limited you may consider including flights in your travel plans. Air New Zealand is the major airline.

TOURS
There are a number of tour operators providing organised tours:
Connections 18–35s: www.connections1835.com.au
Contiki: www.contiki.com.au
Trafalgar Tours: www.trafalgartours.com

JO-JOS
Kiwi Experience offers alternative coach transport for backpackers and independent travellers. It offers several passes which take you 'off the beaten track' and which can easily be purchased once you are in New Zealand through backpacker travel centres. Some allow you to return to where you joined the bus, while others allow you to travel in one direction. It operates on both the North and South islands. There are a number of interestingly named passes: *The Whole Kit and Caboodle* lets you travel the North and South islands; *The Kitchen Sink*, *Gumboot*, *Funky Chicken*, *Stray Dog*, *Sheep Dog*, *Back Paddock*, *Awesome* and *Top Bit and Bottom Bus* to name a few.
Kiwi Experience: www.kiwiexperience.com
170 Parnell Road
Parnell, Auckland, New Zealand
Tel: (09) 366 9830
Fax: (09) 366 1374

Magic Travellers Network offers jo-jos on predetermined routes, including passes to travel both islands; e.g. the *New Zealand North and South*, *New Zealand Magic Adventure*, *New Zealand Navigator*. Other passes allow you to travel only the North (*Northern Discovery*, *Northland Explorer*, *Top of The North*) or South (*Southern Discovery*, *Tranzalpine Experience*, *Wild West Coast*) islands.
Magic Travellers Network: www.magicbus.co.nz
Union House, 136–138 Quay Street
Auckland, New Zealand
Tel: (09) 358 5600
Fax: (09) 358 3471

TRAIN, COACH AND FERRY PASSES
The *Best of New Zealand Pass* offers travellers the opportunity to travel on New Zealand's trains (Tranz Rail), ferries (Interislander and

Lynx Fast Ferry) and coaches (InterCity Coachlines). It works on a points system called Best Points. Each trip you undertake on a train, ferry or coach uses a specific number of points. There are currently three Best Point options available:
- *600 Best Points* which can be used for short breaks or travelling on one island;
- *800 Best Points*;
- *1000 Best Points* which will provide enough points to travel both islands.

All Best Points may be purchased in New Zealand. You can use the train, coach and ferry services separately if you wish.

Great train journeys
The Overlander—Auckland to Wellington and vice versa.
The Geyserland—Auckland to Rotorua and vice versa.
The Coastal Pacific—Christchurch to Picton and vice versa.
The Tranz Alpine—Christchurch to Greymouth and vice versa.
The Southerner—Christchurch to Invercargill and vice versa.

THE OCEANS

Cruising the oceans has had a resurgence in recent years. There are cruise lines which sail the world and there are those that cruise certain areas including the Pacific Islands, Asia, the Caribbean, the Mediterranean, the Greek Islands and Alaska. Pick up brochures on the cruises from your nearest travel agent. Some cruise lines include:

Celebrity Cruise Lines (cruises in Alaska, Bermuda, the Caribbean, Panama and Europe): www.celebrity-cruises.com

Carnival Cruise Lines (cruises in Hawaii, Canada, Panama, Alaska, Bahamas, the Caribbean and Mexico): www.carnival.com

Festival Cruises (cruises in the Canaries, western Mediterranean, the Greek Islands, the Caribbean, Norwegian Fjords and Transatlantic crossings): www.festivalcruises.com

Norwegian Capricorn Line (cruises in the South Pacific and Australasia): www.ncl.com.au

Royal Caribbean International (cruises in the Caribbean, Alaska and the Far East; and Transatlantic crossings): www.rccl.com

Princess Cruises (cruises in Alaska and Canada, Mexico, Panama, Bermuda, the Caribbean, Northern Europe, the Mediterranean, Holy Land, India, Africa, the Orient and Asia, Australia and New Zealand, the South Pacific and round-the-world: www.princess.com

If you are interested in travelling by freighter or cargo ship, there are companies which take passengers. There have been several books published on travelling/working on freighters which you could buy or borrow from a library which may provide freight/cargo company contact details. One website I found, which mentions freighter companies, the nationality of their owners, their sailing schedules and from which port they sail, is: www.freighter-cruises.com

SOUTH-EAST ASIA AND CHINA

For the purposes of this section countries referred to include: Cambodia, China, Hong Kong, Indonesia, Korea, Laos, Malaysia, Myanmar, the Philippines, Singapore, Thailand and Vietnam.

The countries making up the South-East Asian area are diverse. To visit all of these countries and to appreciate what each has to offer would take years, literally. Therefore, you should work out what it is you want to see and experience, then work out the best way to do it, and when to do it. Many travellers decide either to spend a length of time in one country, or link a number of countries together through flights, sea voyages, trains and tours.

It should be noted that each country has its own transport system, including airline/s, buses, trains and local transport such as tuk-tuks, rick-shaws and bemos. During my research I found that there wasn't one place I could go to for information on transport systems. Instead, I had to visit individual country's tourist bureaus for the information and piece it all together myself. I suggest therefore, you do the same or purchase or borrow from the library a specialist travel guide which details the travel options available.

As well as the usual forms of transport I discovered that some countries, such as Malaysia, enable you to travel around the country and into other countries by taxi. Basically, the taxi driver waits until there are four passengers, but you can rent the taxi for yourself as long as you pay for four passengers. Once the taxi is full the driver will take you to where you want to go. You can organise such a taxi trip through hotel receptionists, who can advise you on pricing.

STOPOVERS AND AIR PASSES

Many travellers visit Asian countries as stopovers during long-haul flights between the northern and southern hemispheres. There are therefore a number of stopover packages available in major cities for those only staying a few days. Ask your travel agent about these.

You may wish to incorporate flights into your itinerary to travel around Asia. Most Asian countries have their own airlines, such as, Air China, Cathay Pacific, Garuda Indonesia, Korean Air, Malaysian Airlines, Philippine Airlines, Singapore Airlines and Thai Airways.

TOURS

There are a number of tour companies offering tours to specific countries in this area. There are opportunities to follow routes such as 'The Silk Road' or to trek the Himalayas or pay your respects on a 'war remembrance' tour. See your travel agent for tour brochures. Some specialist tour companies include:

Encounter Overland: www.encounter-overland.com
Intrepid Travel: www.intrepidtravel.com.au
Sundowners (for Trans Siberian): www.sundowners.com.au
World Expeditions: www.worldexpeditions.com.au

TRAINS AND COACHES

Most South-East Asian countries have their own train and coach services. Unfortunately, not all of them link as do the rail and coach services in Europe. However, there are those that do. These include the trains from Singapore, through Malaysia and into Thailand, and vice versa. I was able to pick up timetables for these services at the appropriate tourist bureaus. For example, **KTM** is the train network in Malaysia which offers services to Singapore and Thailand. You can purchase a rail pass for either 10 or 30 days of unlimited travel on KTM inter-city services. Website address: www.ktmb.com.my

The **State Railway of Thailand** has services to major cities including the Northern Line (Bangkok to Chiang Mai), the North-Eastern Line (Bangkok to Nong Khai), the Eastern Line (Bangkok to Aranyaprathet) and the Southern Line (for services into Malaysia and Singapore).

China is a huge country and due to the lengthy distances between major centres the railway system is extensive. There are a number of overnight express trains including those from Kowloon to Shanghai, and vice versa. It is advised that it is far easier for your hotel front desk (once in China) to buy your train ticket as it can be confusing to do it yourself.

Great train journeys

Reunification Express—Hanoi to Saigon (Vietnam) and vice versa.
Trans Siberian—Vladivostok to St Petersburg and vice versa.
Trans Mongolian—Hong Kong via China and Mongolia to St Petersburg, and vice versa.
The Silk Route—Beijing to St Petersburg and vice versa.
Trans Manchurian—Beijing via Manchurian Plains to St Petersburg and vice versa.
The Butterworth Express—Singapore to Bangkok, Thailand.

SEA CRAFT
If you are interested in island hopping, you will be pleased to note that Asian countries are very well serviced by sea cargo routes and ferries. For instance, there are regular services between Hong Kong, China and Japan. From Singapore there are regular ferry services to cities along the Malaysian coast and into Indonesia. Contact ferry and cargo companies in major ports and local tourist offices for details. You may wish to have a look at the freighter website mentioned under 'The Oceans' section.

BICYCLES
Bicycles are a principle form of transport in South-East Asia and China. You could either take your own bike or rent one once you arrive.

UNITED KINGDOM AND REPUBLIC OF IRELAND

The UK (England, Scotland and Wales) and Ireland are extremely popular destinations with extensive rail, coach and road services.

AIR PASSES
The United Kingdom and the Republic of Ireland are very compact countries which makes them easy to get around. However, you may consider including flights in your travel plans. Airlines that service the UK and Ireland and offer point-to-point tickets and air passes include: Aer Lingus, British Airways and British Midland.

TOURS
There are a number of companies which provide coach touring:
Contiki: www.contiki.com
Globus and Cosmos: www.globusandcosmos.com
Insight Tours: www.insighttours.com
Top Deck: www.topdeck.co.uk
Trafalgar Tours: www.trafalgartours.com

As well as the big companies offering organised coach tours, there are a number of smalller firms offering mini-bus tours and jump-on, jump-off touring for independent travellers. You can purchase these tours once you are in the UK. These smaller companies include the following:
Haggis Backpackers offers the choice of three- and six-day tours and jump-on, jump-off touring through Scotland. They also offer a six-day tour of England, Wales and the Scottish Borders.

Haggis Backpackers: www.haggis-backpackers.com
11 Blackfriars Street
Edinburgh EH1 1NB, Scotland
Tel: (0131) 557 9393
Fax: (0131) 558 1177

Hairy Hog specialises in mini-bus tours through Wales.
Hairy Hog: www.hairyhog.co.uk
22 Conduit Place
Paddington, London W2 1HS, United Kingdom
Tel: (020) 7706 1539
Fax: (020) 7706 1538

MacBackpackers offers tours and jo-jos through Scotland.
MacBackpackers: www.macbackpackers.com
105 High Street
Edinburgh EH1 1SG, Scotland
Tel: (0131) 558 9900
Fax: (0131) 220 1869

Outback UK offers 'off-the-beaten-track' tours in England, Scotland and Wales. You can do the full 14-day tour around the UK or explore smaller areas.
Outback UK: www.outbackuk.clara.net
The Cottage, Church Green
Badby, Northants NN11 3AS, United Kingdom
Tel: (01327) 704115

Stray Travel is the backpacker travel network offering tours and passes for travel in England, Scotland, Wales and Ireland.
Stray Travel: www.straytravel.com

London:
171 Earls Court Road
London SW5 9RF, United Kingdom
Tel: (020) 7373 7737
Fax: (020) 7373 7739

Dublin:
6 William Street South
Dublin 1, Eire
Tel: (01) 679 2684
Fax: (01) 670 7740

Tir na nOg Tours (*Tir na nOg* meaning 'Land of Eternal Youth' which is a mythical island off Ireland's west coast where the people remain forever young) offer six-day tours of the southern and northern halves of Ireland. For those on a tight schedule there is a three-day tour of Northern Ireland. All tours depart from Dublin.

Tir na nOg Tours: www.tirnanogtours.com
57 Lower Gardiner Street
Dublin 1, Eire
Tel: (01) 836 4684
Fax: (01) 855 9059

COACH PASSES

National Express is the coach line servicing the UK. As well as providing point-to-point travel to 1200 destinations throughout England, Scotland, Wales and Ireland you can purchase travel passes which include the *Britain Explorer Travel Pass, Scotland Explorer Pass, Ireland Explorer Pass* and the *Europe Explorer Pass* (refer to the coach passes under Europe for more details on this coach line).

You can also purchase a *Tourist Trail Pass* which offers travel within a consecutive period, e.g. two days, unlimited travel within three consecutive days, or seven days, unlimited travel within 21 consecutive days. You can buy these passes once you have arrived in the UK, from the London Coach Terminal, Buckingham Palace Road, London (near Victoria Train Station). Website address: www.nationalexpress.co.uk

Scottish Citylink is the coach service servicing Scotland. Website address: www.citylink.co.uk

TRAIN PASSES

The UK has an extensive rail system serviced by **British Rail**. You can purchase point-to-point tickets once you arrive but if planning to use the network extensively, consider a BritRail Pass. This pass must be bought outside the UK. There are several variations:

BritRail Consecutive Pass gives you unlimited rail travel throughout the UK on consecutive days. Passes are available for 4, 8, 15 and 22 days' or one months' rail travel.

BritRail Flexi Pass which provides travel for 4, 8 or 15 days' travel within a two-month period.

There are also passes for specific areas including the *South East Pass, Freedom of Scotland Pass* and the *BritRail Pass Plus Ireland*.

Both BritRail and Eurail passes allow you to travel Ireland. However, if you only want to travel Ireland you will be pleased to know that Ireland has its own extensive rail and bus systems. For instance, if you only wish to travel in the Republic of Ireland you could purchase an *Irish Explorer* pass, which offers both bus and rail travel or rail travel only for unlimited travel within consecutive days. Or you could purchase an *Irish Rambler*, which offers unlimited travel within consecutive days on buses only.

If you would like to travel in both the Republic of Ireland and Northern Ireland, you may wish to purchase an *Emerald Card*, which allows bus and rail travel. Website address: www.britrail.co.uk

Great train journeys
Eurostar—London to Paris/Brussels and vice versa. Website address: www.eurostar.co.uk

BUYING/SELLING A VEHICLE
Many visitors to the UK purchase a combi van to travel through Europe. Look in the London edition of *TNT* magazine, also in *LOOT* and *Auto Trader*.

There is a van market in London on Market Road, Holloway N7 (the nearest Tube station is Caledonian Road, which is on the Piccadilly Line). Be aware that a lot of these backpacker vehicles have travelled around Europe many times.

SEA CRAFT
The ferries servicing the United Kingdom, Ireland and Europe are large enough to offer a roll-on, roll-off service for those travelling with vehicles and a foot passenger service.
Irish Ferries (between Ireland and Europe): www.irishferries.ie
Stena Sealink Ferries (between the UK, Ireland and the Netherlands): www.stenaline.com

UNITED STATES OF AMERICA

AIR PASSES
As the United States is a large country to travel you may consider including flights in your itinerary. There are a number of major airlines offering air passes. Airlines include: Aloha Air (for Hawaii), American Airlines, America West Airlines, Continental, Delta Airlines, Hawaiian Airlines, TWA, United Airlines, US Airways, etc.

TOURS
There are a number of tour operators which offer organised tours through the USA. There are tours available for the East Coast, West Coast or overland journeys which take you from the East Coast to the West Coast, and vice versa.
Contiki: www.contiki.com
Globus and Cosmos: www.globusandcosmos.com
Insight Tours: www.insighttours.com
Trafalgar Tours: www.trafalgartours.com

Green Tortoise Adventure Travel offers 'stretch-out-and-sleep-while-we-drive' tours. Basically, by day, the coach acts as a normal coach tour taking you to places and allowing you to do things you want to do. By night, the seats turn into bunk beds.

Tours are available in North and Central America. They can be purchased at their main office at the Green Tortoise hostel in San Francisco and at the Green Tortoise hostel in Seattle.

Green Tortoise Adventure Travel: www.greentortoise.com
494 Broadway
San Francisco, CA 94133, USA
Tel: (0415) 834 100

COACH PASSES

The **Greyhound** coach network in the USA is extensive and reaches up to 2600 destinations nationwide. You can purchase an *Ameripass* which offers continuous travel during a set period of days. Passes vary in length and range from seven, 10, 15, 30, 45 and 60 days of travel. Website address: www.greyhound.com

TRAIN PASSES

Amtrak is the national train network in the USA. There are over 500 destinations in the network. Amtrak offer several passes including:
National Rail Pass, which allows unlimited stopovers within 15 or 30 days of travel when travelling from coast to coast.
Far West Rail Pass, which allows travel within the western states.
West Rail Pass, which allows travel within western states to the mid-west.
Northeast Rail Pass, which allows travel in the north-eastern region.
East Rail Pass, which allows travel in the eastern states.
Coastal Rail Passes, which allows travel within the East or West coasts.
North American Rail Pass, which allows travel in Canada.
Website address: www.amtrak.com

DRIVE-AWAYS

In the USA there is the possibility of doing a drive-away. This is when you deliver a private car within the USA. Some Americans prefer to drive their own car while on holidays but do not wish to drive it to the actual starting point themselves. This is where you come in. There are companies which can arrange for you to deliver the car to this initial destination by a specified date. You will get free use of the car but will be required to pay for the gas.

If you are interested in doing this, look up 'Drive-away Companies' or 'Automobile Transporters' in the US Yellow Pages.

TRAVEL ALONE

It seems the most common reason why people sacrifice their dream of living, working and playing overseas is that they don't want to go alone. Yes, it can be scary, yes, you may sometimes feel uneasy, especially when dining alone, and yes, you will feel vulnerable—but don't let these concerns put you off. In fact, I have often found travelling with someone else to be a hindrance. This is because when I am travelling with other people I tend to remain with them, but when I am travelling on my own I make a more concerted effort to meet other people. Still, be selective and wary of strangers. If you are worried about travelling alone, here are some tips:

- Look approachable. Smile at other travellers, let them know you don't mind being distracted from staring out of that window or from the book you are reading.
- Don't feel self-conscious about speaking to the person sitting next to you on the plane, train or bus, because you might just make a friend. If you do make an idiot of yourself, who cares? You will probably never see them again anyway.
- Stay at hostels as these are full of travellers. Many are on their own and looking for friends.
- Ask that room mate what they are doing for their next meal. Maybe you could have a meal together, or sightsee.
- Join in activities at hostels. Even if it is only watching TV—someone might be watching their favourite show which could be yours as well. Discuss what is happening during the ads.
- Join the travel clubs mentioned in this guide and participate in the activities they organise.
- Book an organised tour with a company who specialises in tours for a certain age group, like 18 to 30-something, because many single travellers take these not only to see the sights but to meet other like-minded travellers.
- Employment agencies sometimes have get-togethers for their temps; go along and meet other temps.
- On work assignments, if asked to go for a drink, go.
- If someone has given you the phone number of a friend of a friend of a friend, give them a call—you have nothing to lose.
- If someone hasn't seen their relatives in years, maybe offer to pay their family a visit to pass on the latest news. They in turn might pass on tips about finding accommodation or job opportunities. They could even offer a meal or put you up.

So get up and go, even if it is by yourself, because you won't be by yourself for long. And you'll regret it if you don't do it.

TRAVEL SAFE

Civil wars, famine, volcanic eruptions, floods and fires are just a few of the things happening in countries around the world. If you are travelling to a country where your safety may be at risk, then you can obtain travel warnings from government bodies such as the two mentioned below. They can advise on destinations to avoid and any dangers to watch out for. Website addresses:

The Department of Foreign Affairs (Australia): www.dfat.com.au
US State Dept: Travel Warnings: //travel.state.gov/travel_warnings.html

Looking like a tourist means you may attract unsavoury types so try to blend in, which can be pretty hard if you have fair skin and blonde hair in a country where people are predominantly dark-haired and dark-skinned, or vice versa. Unfortunately, there are some unscrupulous people in the world who like to target travellers.

Of course, you want to visit the tourist spots, but cameras and maps identify you as a tourist. If possible, try to keep cameras and maps out of sight until needed. Study the place you are going to before you get there, so you look like you know where you're going and what you're doing (even if you don't!).

Be careful of the way you carry bags. They can easily be slit open without your knowing if they are slung over your back. A suggestion is to wear the bag with the bulk of it in front of you. If you find this annoying maybe you should not carry a large bag at all. Girls could wear a small shoulder bag worn with the strap draped diagonally over the body and the purse part in front. Don't wear it slung over the shoulder as moped drivers have been known to grab bags and speed off in seconds. Keep it secure on your person. You could wear it under your jacket so the strap can't be grabbed.

If you decide to use a money belt, don't expose it when a lot of people are around. Have funds for the day readily available somewhere else, like a pocket. Wearing a bum bag can indicate that this is where you have all your valuables. For this reason, travellers nowadays are preferring not to wear them. If you must wear a bum bag, make sure it is secure and facing forward.

Do not ever leave your bag unattended or let it out of your sight. Two friends were once asked by another tourist for directions. As they looked at his map he moved them around so their backs were to their bags which, of course, was a ploy so an accomplice could steal their bags. The tourist then disappeared very fast.

With backpacks, take them off and put them in front of you as soon as possible. When in crowded public transport try to lean against a wall so no one can unzip any pockets.

You should be conscious at all times of where your valuables are. Don't put wallets in back pockets as they can easily be snatched. If a commotion breaks out around you, hold your valuables and move away as quickly as possible. Once, on a main street in Istanbul, two cars parked on the footpath blocked most of the way. When a group of unsuspecting tourists, one being myself, had to get into single file to make it past the cars, a commotion broke out around us and one guy almost lost his wallet. Be aware of what is going on around you.

Try to stay in populated areas because that dark, lonely back street might prove fatal. It is strongly advised not to leave valuables in hostel rooms. It is sad to say, but sometimes it's other travellers that you need to be wary of.

Be wary of female beggars with young children as they can give you the child to nurse and while you're goo-ing and gah-ing over the child an accomplice may take your valuables.

At automated bank machines be aware of who is behind you. A Japanese girl I met was taking money out of the machine and someone reached over her, grabbed her money and ran off.

When at work, keep your belongings close to you. With any luck there will be lockers or a lockable drawer to put your things in. Temporary office workers are often placed at someone else's desk which doesn't leave much room for your things.

If you don't trust the door to your accommodation, put something against it which will make a noise if someone tries to enter.

Don't go into parks and gardens after dark. A friend once went to the pub after being paid, flashed his money around and was mugged in a park on his way home.

As mentioned under 'Packing' in Chapter 1, make sure you dress appropriately in countries with dress codes. Girls should be careful when travelling alone in these countries because you may receive unwanted attention. Dress conservatively as you might trigger male primitive instincts or the green-eyed monster in other females.

Be careful when approached by locals, particularly those who offer food or drink or invite you to join them for a drink. There have been cases where unsuspecting travellers accept the offer and find themselves waking up hours later with their valuables missing.

Be careful when accepting lifts from strangers as they could easily take you to a lonely place, rob you, or worse, hold you hostage.

If asked to participate in a (friendly) game of poker, or any game involving betting, be wary. Some games are organised and you may end up owing thousands—and you will be escorted to the bank to get the money or receive grievous bodily harm.

Being offered great deals is another scam; e.g. being offered a great price on gems, only to find out later they are fake. Another scam involves a stranger telling you that you have something on your shirt like bird droppings or sauce. They offer to remove the offending spot, only to remove your valuables also. There have also been cases of travellers being gassed during overnight train journeys where thieves have rifled through belongings while you are knocked out. This is why some travellers take turns with their companion to take 'first watch'. Others ensure they leave a window open.

These examples show the ways in which thieves work, so be wary. Heed any advice or warnings given on safety because it may happen to you. If anything does happen, hopefully you will have a list elsewhere of important numbers and photocopies of relevant documents. Your Consulate can offer assistance if you lose your passport, get arrested, robbed or assaulted, etc. Contact your Consulate before you leave to learn exactly what services are offered.

Some Consulates suggest that if you intend to stay in another country for an extended stay you should register your contact details with the Consulate. Then, if an emergency arises (at home for instance), the Consulate will be able to locate you.

TRAVEL WELL
Vaccinations

Depending on where you're travelling, you may need vaccinations. See your doctor or a specialist travel medical centre for the proper innoculations before departing. It wouldn't hurt (no pun intended) to have your childhood injections boosted, plus hepatitis A, polio and tetanus. Have these a few months before departure in case you have adverse reactions or need a booster shot. Ensure you receive a vaccination certificate as some countries require them before they will let you enter. Nurses and those in medical fields are advised to carry their immunisation details if they hope to work overseas.

For a comprehensive picture of the world's health, take a look at the WHO (World Health Organisation) website: www.who.ch

Coping with long-haul travel

LONG-HAUL PLANE TRAVEL
Some travellers experience jetlag after long-haul air travel, while others have to cope with air sickness even on short flights.

If you've never flown before or just feel anxious about it, avoid drinking stimulants such as coffee, tea and alcohol. Drink calming chamomile tea (take your own on the plane) or take a non-addictive herbal relaxant such as valerian. If your ears pop during landing and take-off, swallowing helps, as does sucking a lolly (sweet).

Even though it is preferred that you stay in your seat during the flight (in case of sudden turbulence), get up and move around occasionally. Sitting for long periods of time inhibits circulation.

Simple exercises done in your seat help improve circulation. Starting with your feet, rotate your ankles in both directions then stretch and wiggle your toes. Press your knees together and tighten your buttocks. Pull in your stomach. Rotate your wrists. Stretch and shake your fingers out. Rotate your shoulders; raise them up and down then backwards and forwards. Slowly rotate your neck. Have a big stretch. Try these on long bus and train journeys, along with other exercises you invent. You might get funny looks, or start a trend. Sleeping, between contortions, is the hardest thing to do on a plane, or in a bus, train or car, for that matter. You may want to invest in an inflatable pillow to support your neck. Maybe a prescribed sleeping tablet will help you.

Avoid alcohol and drink plenty of water so you don't dehydrate. Spend a little time on the plane pampering yourself by cleaning your teeth, brushing your hair, washing your face and applying liberal amounts of moisturiser. All these things will make you feel fresher.

Many travellers break a long trip with a stopover because, as those who suffer from sinus problems might appreciate, exposure to long periods of pressurised cabin air can cause the nose to become dried out and stuffy. In my case, long flights can make my nose bleed; this happens to a lot of people.

People who wear contact lenses might want to wear glasses for a long flight as cabin air dries your eyes. A stopover helps alleviate jetlag and other effects associated with flying, like swollen ankles.

When you reach your destination, try not to sleep until the evening so your body adjusts to the new time zone. Easier said than done, I know. Go for a walk or to the gym for exercise. Take a long rehydrating bath or shower and apply plenty of moisturiser. You may want to put tea bags on your eyes to reduce puffiness. Try inverted posture to cure swollen ankles. If on arrival none of these suggestions have made you feel 'alive' again, you could go out, get drunk, then blame it on the hangover which you know you'll recover from!

Only time will tell if you travel well or not. Hopefully most of us have grown out of travel sickness, but for those who suffer there are preparations available, so see your chemist, doctor or health food shop. Prevention is the best method.

LONG-HAUL TRAIN AND COACH TRAVEL
For long distances, some people prefer train travel as they can get up and walk through the carriages to stretch their legs. Another advantage of train travel is staying in a sleeper compartment.

If travelling by bus, it is wise to get out and stretch your legs each time the bus stops. Just like flying, with lack of exercise your feet can swell. Do take some munchies and a drink for long coach trips because stops at roadhouses and diners can prove costly for the budget-conscious traveller.

Some people take overnight coach and train travel to avoid paying for accommodation. Some expect to get a decent night's sleep before disembarking in the morning. Unfortunately, it doesn't always work like this. You may not get any sleep because of poor-quality beds or seats and dubious co-travellers. Also, depending on the arrival time, accommodation at your destination may be closed, and you may not be allowed to sleep at the train or coach station.

Sea travel

It is highly possible that sea travel will be included in your travels. Even on calm seas people have been known to get sick, so prevention is the best method. People use a number of methods, including staying on deck in the fresh air. Others opt for preparations which can be bought from chemists such as tablets, bracelets and patches that are strategically placed on certain areas of your body.

Eating well on the road

Even the best cast-iron stomachs can react badly to foreign foods. The best advice is to eat new things in moderation, and take antacid.

Some tour companies, particularly the ones catering to young people, often make a point of having drinks at the bar on arrival at your accommodation each night before dinner. If your nutrition is suffering due to this alcoholic regime, take a multi-vitamin supplement or ration your booze intake.

One health problem with travelling on coach tours is that if one person gets a cold, many of the others will catch it soon enough.

Unfortunately, the fun can 'run' out of your holiday if you are struck by the most common health problem which effects travellers. Often referred to as Bali Belly (and other bellies), Mexican two-step or Rangoon Runs—yes, we're talking diarrhoea.

Diarrhoea can be attributed to different water, unfamiliar food, a new environment or spicy foods, but is mainly caused by eating food and drinking water contaminated with bacteria.

Diarrhoea usually occurs within the first week or so of a trip, but the most frustrating thing is that it can occur at any time. In most cases diarrhoea clears up within a few days with a little treatment.

You may consider travelling with a non-prescription tablet available at chemists if you are worried.

Also remember to drink only bottled water, especially if you're ill.

Don't be paranoid about trying the local food for fear of becoming sick, just be careful and selective.

Note that if you have special dietary requirements (kosher or vegetarian, for example), then advise the airline or tour company beforehand so they can arrange appropriate meals.

An STD-free holiday

The motto 'be prepared' is sound advice, and in most cases travellers are very well prepared. After all, we read travel guides to learn more about our destinations, we shop around for bargains, we take out holiday insurance, we have vaccinations, we purchase backpacks and hiking boots to make our travel more comfortable, and we pack all those very important might-use knick-knacks like traveller's washing powder, adaptor plugs, money belts and mosquito nets. We even heed safety advice and only drink bottled water and avoid food from suspect-looking places. Yes, we travellers are very well prepared, but are we truly ready for everything? What about SEX?

One thing most of us forget to pack are condoms. But why would you need them when you're travelling? After all, you're going for scenery and life experience and not, I mean *not*, travelling to meet someone, right? What happens if you do meet someone? Do you ignore them because you refuse to have unprotected sex? No, you grab that chance, don't you? I mean, when will you have sex on a snowy part of the Himalayas again or on the French Riviera, right? But there is nowhere to buy condoms so, after a few drinks, the two of you crawl into one sleeping bag and greet the new day as a couple. In the morning you wonder if you should have used protection!

If you think this won't happen to you, well think again, it happens quite often and some of us can be left with unwanted friends. The most common unwanted friends are STDs (sexually transmitted diseases), which include chlamydia, gonorrhoea, herpes, hepatitis B, syphilis and the HIV virus. Some may even cause long-term effects such as infertility if left untreated.

Some STDs are more prevalent in certain areas. For instance, South-East Asia has a more resistant form of gonorrhoea. Seek medical advice on the best ways to avoid STDs in this area and others.

Diseases such as Hepatitis B and HIV can be spread through skin penetration so tattooing, acupuncture and body piercing should be avoided. Or ensure that any needles and syringes used are sterile.

The best advice for travellers (single or not) is be prepared and pack condoms even if you don't plan to have sex, because you just might, and you don't want to come home with any unwanted friends.

Women travelling alone, safe and well

Some societies have an attitude towards women that differs greatly to what you are used to. This can make it hard and sometimes dangerous for women to travel on their own. No matter your feelings on the subject, you will need to be more culturally sensitive when travelling in these countries.

Some tips: travel with a male friend; know local dress customs; cover up to avoid unwanted attention; wear a wedding ring to make it look like you 'belong to someone'; and be aware of laws on drinking alcohol in public places.

There are, however, advantages to being a woman travelling alone. In some cases it is far easier to obtain work.

Girls taking oral contraception should watch out for the time difference and have a supply of sanitary wear available. Some girls take oral contraceptives continuously to avoid having their periods while travelling. This is something to consider.

LIVE, WORK AND PLAY'S BUDGET TRAVEL TIPS

- Take advantage of public transport, including purchasing travel passes. Use public transport to and from the airport.
- Only have breakfast at the hotel if it is included in the price. If it is, request extra bread rolls which you could take for lunch.
- Purchase food items (coffee, tea bags, etc.) from a supermarket and carry them with you.
- Refill your water bottle instead of purchasing drinks.
- Visit all the free tourist attractions. There are, however, some things that need to be experienced, regardless of the price tag.
- Be aware of the exchange rate and obtain the best available.
- Don't make phone calls from hotel rooms. Purchase prepaid phonecards and make calls during off-peak times.
- Order lunch and dinner specials of the day.
- Travel during off-peak times rather than peak times.

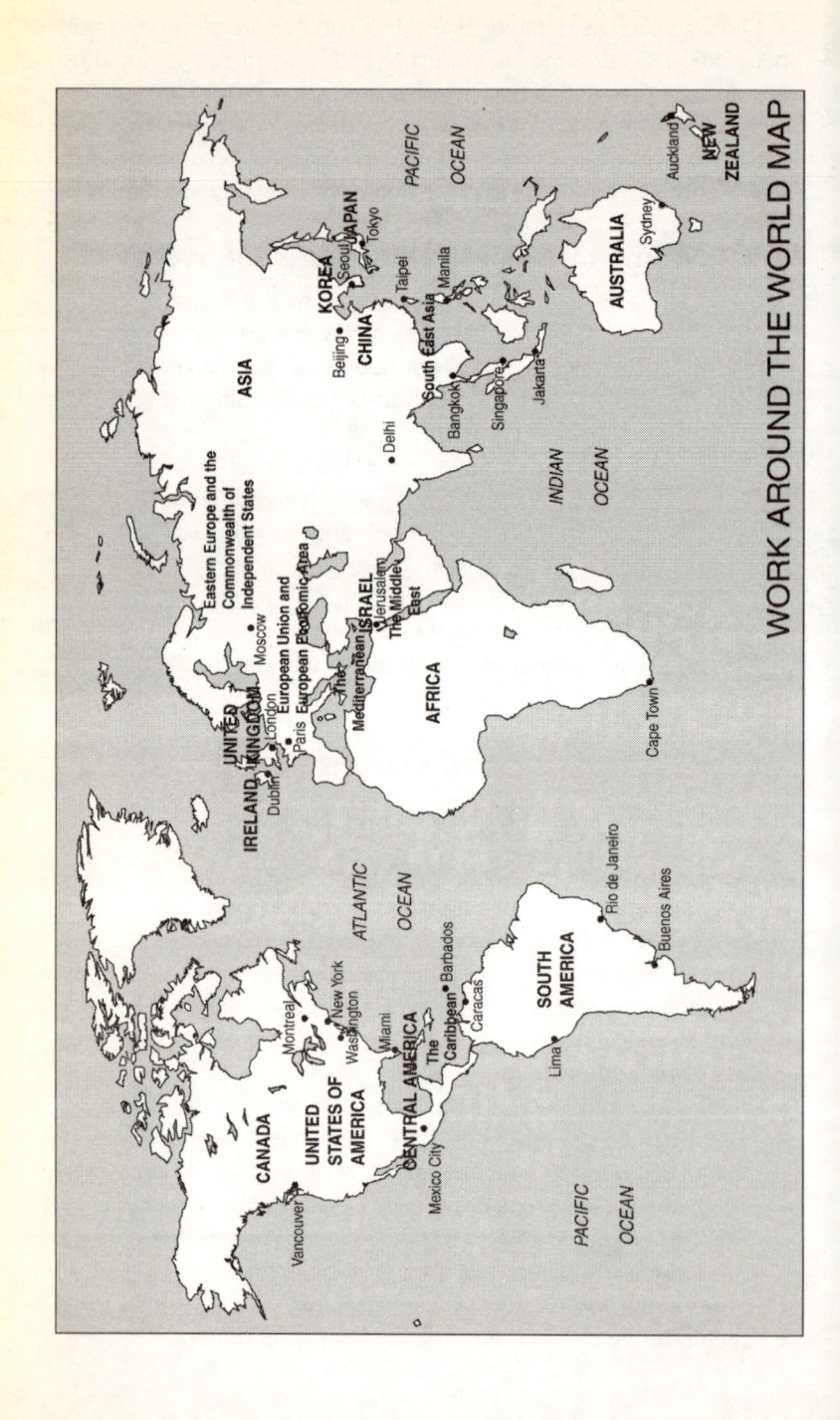

WORK AROUND THE WORLD MAP

PART TWO

CHAPTER 5
Work

Travellers who want to work in other countries around the world can do so:
- by going on an official working holiday scheme;
- by going on a pre-arranged work program;
- by finding an employer who will agree to sponsor you, for example, contract positions;
- by securing cash work after arrival;
- by being transferred by your current employer, although this option is really for a lucky few (if you currently work for a company with offices in many countries, there may be opportunities for you to be transferred to one of its overseas offices, usually the company will organise the appropriate visa for you);
- by travelling on a student visa which allows you to undertake part-time work (usually up to 20 hours per week).

WORKING HOLIDAY SCHEMES

A working holiday scheme involves a country issuing a visa which allows young people to live and work—and play—in that country, usually for one to two years. These let you experience another culture while earning some money to fund further travels. A visa for a working holiday scheme is only ever issued once in your lifetime and you should take full advantage of the allowed length of stay.

A country with a working holiday scheme stipulates the criteria which individuals must meet to qualify for the visa. Information on these schemes is provided under the appropriate country in the Area Analysis chapter. In general though, you must:
- be aged within the set age limit, which varies for individual countries and is often between the ages of 18 and 26, and in some cases up to the age of 30;
- very importantly, be taking a holiday in the country and only seek work that is incidental to provide funds to further your travels;

- only undertake specific work, which should be advised in the information supplied to you before you apply for the visa (some countries do not have such restrictions);
- have sufficient funds in your bank account to prove you can support yourself during your initial stay (this amount is set by the individual countries and can be influenced by exchange rates);
- register as an 'alien' within a specific time of arrival in the country and apply for the relevant tax number, etc.;
- undertake a medical examination;
- attend an interview;
- provide a letter stating why you want to live and work in that country;
- have no criminal record;
- agree to leave at the end of your authorised stay.

Do check if there is a visa application fee and whether the visa is a single-entry or multiple-entry type. Also check whether you must apply for the working holiday visa in your home country or can apply for it in another country during your travels.

Contact the individual Consulates and Embassies nearest to you for the appropriate details. In some cases you can download this information from the Internet, including application forms.

PROGRAMS

Working holiday programs are different from the schemes outlined above. Some act as an assistance service only and do not find you a specific position or arrange a visa, while others, such as summer camps in the USA and Au Pair Programs, do. You will be required to pay to go on these programs but the cost involved can include:
- your airfare (optional);
- help with obtaining the appropriate visa;
- a guaranteed position for a specific period with a weekly salary;
- accommodation (or advice on where to find it);
- meals (this depends on the individual program);
- extras including guide books and T-shirts;
- orientation and support before and during the program.

A number of organisations offer these programs. Here is a selection of programs and organisations:

Au Pair Programs—A number of countries, including the United States and many European nations, allow people to enter their country to spend time with a local family as an au pair.

Being an au pair is regarded by authorities as a cultural experience because you are not only looking after children but are experiencing another country's way of life. Thus, countries will issue cultural exchange visas (these visas have different names in different countries but are issued under the premise of a cultural exchange visa and not a working visa) to those wishing to be au pairs.

Companies that can help you find a position are listed under the 'Nanny, mother's help and au pair positions' section in Chapter 7.

The Council on International Educational Exchange (Council) was founded in 1947. It has been operating work and study programs for over 25 years. Its mission is 'to help people gain understanding, acquire knowledge and develop skills for living in a globally interdependent and culturally diverse world'.

Council offer a number of Work and Travel assistance programs. These programs provide an assistance service and support during all the stages of your trip. It can answer all your questions before you leave as well as offer competitive prices on flights, travel passes, insurance, accommodation, ISIC card, etc. On arrival at your destination, you will receive a comprehensive orientation. Throughout your stay there is a full back-up service.

Work and Travel programs are available for: Australia, Canada, Costa Rica, France, Germany, the Netherlands, Ireland, Japan, New Zealand, the United Kingdom and the USA. It should be noted that you can only participate on a program if you qualify for the appropriate working holiday visa.

Council also offers a number of other programs:

Internship USA—operates throughout the year. Participants, in conjunction with their employer, choose when they want to go. They can work in the USA for up to 18 months and must secure their job prior to departure to the USA. Participants need to be current full-time university or TAFE students, recent graduates or deferred from their course. Council sponsors the USA work visa and provides direct access to over 18,000 employers via their live database.

Teach English in China—involves teaching English to local elementary, college or tertiary students. No Chinese language or teaching experience is required. Participants must only hold a Bachelor degree in any discipline. Council finds the teaching placement and the institution provides accommodation and salary. Council provides intensive teaching training and orientation on arrival in Beijing. Participants can choose between either a five- or 10-month contract, with departures taking place in early March or early September.

Language Programs—Council offers nine locations to study in France, Spain, Italy or Germany. Participants choose the course level to suit their needs from 'standard' to 'intensive', or individual courses in small classes of up to 10 people. Classes are undertaken exclusively at Language Plus schools which are ideally equipped and in appropriate surroundings for leisure and cultural activities.

For comprehensive details of all of Council's programs contact one of the offices mentioned below or look at its website.

The Council on International Educational Exchange (Council): www.councilexchanges.org

Australia	Tel: (02) 9373 2730
China	Tel: (010) 6275 1287
France	Tel: (01) 44 41 74 74
Germany	Tel: (0228) 98 36 00
Ireland	Tel: (01) 602 1777
Italy	Tel: (06) 683 2109
Japan	Tel: (03) 5467 5501
Spain	Tel: (034) 1532 2310
Taiwan	Tel: (02) 8780 2324
Thailand	Tel: (02) 254 8210
UK	Tel: (020) 7478 2000
USA	Tel: (0212) 822 2600

International Agricultural Exchange Association (IAEA) can help place those with genuine experience in agriculture and horticulture between the ages of 18 and 30 in many European countries, Japan, Canada, the USA, Australia and New Zealand. For full details refer to the 'Agriculture and farming' section in Chapter 7.

Holiday camps—Every year, families and children head off to holiday camps. The most popular and widely known camps are the summer camps in the USA. As the USA does not have a working holiday visa available, one way for travellers to live, work and play in the USA is to go on a Summer Camp program. There are, however, many other holidays camps where travellers find positions. These include camps in Europe, the UK and the Republic of Ireland. For details refer to the 'Holiday camps' section in Chapter 7.

International Exchange Programs (IEP), in association with BUNAC (British Universities North American Club) and the YMCA of the USA and Australia, has been offering work/travel programs since 1962. Current programs include:

Summer Camp USA—a popular program for 19- to 35-year-olds for a 10-week summer in the USA. You receive pocket money as well as food and board while on camp. IEP is looking for people who love working with children and have a skill relevant to camp all over the USA. Applications are accepted between September and May for the upcoming season, which commences in June.

Work USA—this program is for full-time TAFE and university students (of any age) who must be studying the year they want to apply (including deferred and students graduating). This program lets you work for four months from November to March in several positions in the USA, including ski resorts. Applications are accepted between April and September each year for November departures.

OPT USA—this traineeship program is for anyone wanting to take up work in the USA for a period of three to 18 months. The position must be organised by the participant and must be relevant to your career, i.e. it must enhance your career. There is no age limit. Some career fields are not eligible. Applications are accepted all year round.

Work & Travel Britain—this program provides support to those who are already intending to travel to the UK for a working holiday. You must already qualify for a working holiday visa, ancestry visa or have a British passport to take advantage of this program. IEP assists with departures, finding a job, accommodation and provides orientations in the UK at their London and Edinburgh offices. There are regular pub meets, tours and parties as well as mail forwarding and a resource centre for all program participants. The program helps people find their feet once they arrive in the UK to work.

Work Australia—this program operates for those from the USA, the UK, the Netherlands, Denmark and Canada who want to come to Australia. IEP provides arrival support, accommodation, a job-finding service, mail forwarding, emergency assistance and ongoing support in Australia.

For more information on programs, contact your nearest office:
Australia—Contact IEP, Tel: 1300 300 912, website address: www.iep-australia.com
Canada—Contact SWAP, Tel: (0416) 966 2887, website address: www.swap.ca
Denmark—Contact EXIS, Tel: (0457) 4429749, website address: www.exis.dk
Netherlands—Contact Travel Active, Tel: (0478) 551900, website address: www.travelactive.nl
New Zealand—Contact IEP, Tel: (09) 366 6255, website address: www.iepnz.co.nz

United Kingdom—Contact BUNAC, Tel: (020) 7251 3472, website address: www.bunac.org.uk

USA—Contact BUNAC, Tel: (0203) 264 0901, website address: www.bunac.org.uk

Volunteer work and programs—Most people, when they think of volunteering, firstly think of aid work, helping victims of natural disasters or wars. There are, however, a number of other volunteer options, including volunteering on conservation projects, archaeological digs, fund-raising, and working with the poor, disabled, orphaned or elderly. For more details, refer to the 'Volunteer work and programs' section in Chapter 7.

SPONSORSHIP

Finding a company which will sponsor you to work overseas can be a long process. This is because the company must prove that there is no national in its country that can fill the position. Once this is proved, then someone from overseas can be offered the position.

If, however, you can teach English, you can gain sponsorship from a school. For more details refer to the 'Teaching' section in Chapter 7.

SECURING CASH WORK AFTER YOUR ARRIVAL

Travellers without legal work documents can sometimes find cash work. An alternative to this is to trade your services for accommodation and meals.

When you do not have the appropriate work visa and are working for cash, you are at the mercy of your employer. Before you begin work, ensure you establish your rate of pay and, more importantly, when you will be paid. It is suggested that you arrange to be paid on a weekly basis. Otherwise, if the employer reneges on your cash-work agreement (which will be verbal) and takes advantage of you, you have no recourse to lodge a complaint.

Also, consider the work environment. Is it clean and safe? What would you do if you are injured while working? In all likelihood, you would have to cover your own medical expenses.

Countries have tightened up on illegal workers. Authorities have been known to make raids for illegal workers in popular 'cash work areas', such as tourist and agricultural regions. Severe fines are imposed on employers employing illegal workers. Illegal employees can be fined, jailed or deported.

Where there are chronic labour shortages, such as in fruit and vegetable areas, farmers may turn a blind eye to your lack of appropriate paperwork only because they need their crop harvested. Authorities may (and I stress *may*) also turn a blind eye to illegal workers.

If you are worried about being caught, trade your services in return for accommodation and food. Trading your services means you are not really breaking any laws, because you are not receiving any income for the work you are doing.

I remember being in Greece and a travelling companion offered his services to paint the pension we were staying in. He stayed an extra week on the island of Crete by doing this. And yes, there was time for him to play!

It is worth noting that you should dress appropriately when you are 'door-knocking', as first impressions count. If you are visiting language schools, for example, you don't have to wear corporate dress, but at least have a wash, shave and dress neatly.

Although door-knocking has proved fruitful for many travellers, it can also be depressing if you continuously have doors slammed in your face. You must therefore remain positive and motivated in your search for work. It can be worth your while to visit the establishments on a number of occasions. This could be every day for a week or more. Persistence can pay off!

Sometimes, you need to be in the right place to find work, so look at where you are and adapt your skills according to the region you are in. For instance:
- holiday centres (beach, ski resorts)—hospitality work;
- major city, town or regional centre—office support, accounting, hospitality, labouring, etc.;
- industrial town—trade positions;
- mining town—trade positions, hospitality;
- farming community—fruit and vegetable picking and farm work.

Sometimes you also need to arrive at the right time of the year to find work. For instance, beach resorts will have more opportunities during summer (life guards, pool attendants, hospitality), while ski resorts will yield more opportunities during winter. At Christmas time there may be retail positions in shops. Santa Clauses and Santa's helpers are also needed. Therefore, timing can mean everything.

In general, travellers find work because they are flexible and willing to do, and try, most things. Travellers often take the positions locals don't want because they know these positions are short-term and they will yield quick funds to further future travels.

There are two things that let travellers down, and they are commitment and reliability. Yes, you are on holiday to enjoy yourself, which employers realise, but if you find work you will be expected to work for the period you commit yourself to. There are some travellers who will only work until they make enough money to take off. This has unfortunately meant that in some professions job-hunting travellers have a bad reputation. For instance, some who find work on a prawn trawler off the coast of Australia think it is a holiday on a boat in the sun. Not so, and many captains do not like employing travellers for this reason. If you take on a position, fulfil your commitment. Future working holidaymakers are depending on you to keep work opportunities available.

OPTIONS FOR FINDING WORK

As mentioned previously, finding work can depend on your visa status. If you are on a working holiday scheme you are generally allowed to take up any form of employment, though there are some restrictions as to what work you can undertake. You could contact employment agencies in your specialist field before you arrive.

If you are on a program, you will be expected to undertake the specific work of that program, for example as an au pair for a family or 'counselor' on a summer camp. If you do not have the appropriate work visa, you may be limited to cash-work opportunities. These are best found by door-knocking or through word of mouth from fellow travellers. Here are some other options for finding work.

The Internet

The popularity of the Internet sees many companies and organisations creating their own website to advertise their products and services. I highly recommend the Internet to source information and contacts, not only for work opportunities, but information on all sorts of things related to your travels, including accommodation, tour companies, travel gear, travel agents and travel literature.

I found the Internet extremely useful and superior to most other forms of contact when sourcing the organisations to include in this guide. For instance, when I rang some of the programs for information, it took some days, sometimes weeks, for the information to arrive.

By using the Internet, up-to-date information was readily available on the program's website. This included general information, positions available and employment conditions. Many positions could be applied for on-line.

Also, sourcing overseas contacts was made much easier through the Internet. I did not have to wait weeks for information to arrive in the mail. Email and faxing took care of that. Therefore if you do not currently have access to the Internet, I would strongly suggest you spend some time at a library or an Internet cafe.

I have included as many website addresses in this travel guide as possible. They are mentioned under the appropriate sections.

There are a couple of general work websites on the Internet which are worth having a look at, and they are discussed below.

The **Careermosaic** site allows you to search for positions and profiles on hundreds of employers. There are links to Careermosaic sites in North America, Europe, Asia and Australia. Website address: www.careermosaic.com

The site also has links to specific industry sites, including:
Accounting positions: www.accountingjobs.com
Health positions: www.healthjobs.com
Insurance positions: www.insjobs.com

The **Monsterboard** site has hundreds of jobs listed from around the world. You can link to Monsterboard sites in other countries where you can localise your search:
Australia and New Zealand: www.monsterboard.com.au
Belgium: www.monster.be
Canada (in French and English): www.monster.ca
Netherlands: www.monsterboard.nl
United Kingdom: www.monsterboard.co.uk
USA: www.monsterboard.com

Employment/recruitment agencies

Many people find work through specialist employment/recruitment agencies.

Before the recession of the 1980s, employers hired temporaries to cover staff shortages and work overloads. Since then, employers have realised they can reduce overheads by keeping permanent staff to a minimum and relying on temporaries and contractors. A large number of specialist employment agencies now exist to supply qualified and experienced temporaries and contractors to employers. This is excellent news for work-seeking travellers. If you have never worked through an employment agency before, here is a quick rundown on how they work.

First, contact an agency. It can be difficult choosing an agency to register with because of their competing claims—they'll all say they are 'the biggest' and/or 'the longest established' and/or 'the best'.

Agencies can also function differently from country to country. For instance, government regulations can mean that employment agencies can either specialise in placing people in permanent or casual work, but not both. Then there are those employment agencies which are allowed to do both.

Most employment agencies offer a free service to employees—they charge the employer. There are some agencies in certain countries who can, and do, charge you a job-finding fee. Some agencies are tucked away in high-rise buildings and require you to make an appointment before they will see you. Others, such as those in the UK, have shopfronts where they advertise positions in their window and which allow you to walk in off the street and ask about the advertised work. Some employment agencies are small with one office in one city in the world or operate from the owner's house. Others are multinational companies. These agencies will often allow you to register with an office in one city for work and will transfer your details to another office in another country to await your arrival to help find you work. On arrival, you contact the agency and advise them of your availability for work.

Once you have chosen an agency, be prepared to 'sell yourself' during this initial introduction by stressing your strengths. For example, 'I have two years' experience using advanced functions on W4W'; 'I have been in A&E of a major city hospital for three years'; 'I have trade certificates and have been plumbing for five years.' Got the idea?

You should be advised of what to bring to the interview (if not, ask). Usually it will be your updated CV, references and original or notarised copies of your qualifications and certificates. They will also require your bank account details so they can pay any salary directly into your account (if you do not have an account, the agency can advise you how to open one and may even ask their bankers to open one for you), your passport showing proof you have the appropriate work documentation, and your tax number so that you will be taxed correctly. If you haven't applied for a tax number, the agency should be able to advise you where and how to obtain this.

You will need to physically register with the agency or agencies as no agency will give you work over the phone. Agencies vary as to how formal or informal they can be. For instance, financial recruitment agencies will be more formal than, say, a labouring employment agency. You will be required to dress appropriately for the interview for the type of work you are seeking, for example, corporate dress for financial positions.

Be honest and tell the consultant what your skills are. Agencies will test these skills (e.g. a typing test, software-package knowledge test, table test for croupiers) to prove you have them and so they can place you in an appropriate position. Do not let an agency bully you into accepting a position you know you cannot do. Some agencies will do this just to fill the position.

Keeping your consultant up-to-date with your availability is imperative, so keep in contact with them. Try to call in at least once a day, preferably in the morning so that if a job comes in (which most do in the morning as employees ring in ill) you are fresh in their mind.

The length of time from registering with the agency until you are offered work can vary greatly. It has been known for people to be offered a position on the spot. Others have waited a day or a week for a position. It is wise to initially register with a few agencies to give yourself the best advantage of obtaining work. Some agencies like you to come and 'sit in' in the office (particularly on a Monday morning) and wait for work. This isn't as absurd as it sounds. I have done it myself and found it very fruitful. If you are ready and waiting for work, the consultant can send you directly to the position.

You will definitely need a contact number if you are going to work through an agency. As soon as a position comes in (which can be at any time) the consultant will ring around to fill it, and if you cannot be contacted, the job will go to someone else.

When agencies are offering you an assignment they should go through some details with you first. They should tell you the nature of the position, the skills required, some background information on the company and, most importantly, the rate of pay (temporaries and contractors are paid on an hourly rate). If you accept the position, they will give you the full address, directions on how to get there and the contact name of the person you are to report to.

At the end of the day or week you will be required to fill in a timesheet showing how many hours you have worked. If you do not have a timesheet you can list your hours on a company letterhead. This is required to be signed by your supervisor for the length of the assignment. Once signed, your timesheet or letterhead is given or faxed to your agency which then pays you accordingly.

If you are offered a contract, make sure you read it carefully. Some employers may say 'this is a standard contract', which can imply that there is nothing wrong with the contract, but it is likely to be drafted to the employer's advantage. Therefore, before you sign anything, make sure you are fully aware of the implications of each clause. Don't be afraid to negotiate.

Government-run employment agencies

Most countries have a central employment network. Although these have been set up to help the unemployed of that country, many of them can, and do, help travellers find positions. They can particularly help with seasonal work during fruit and vegetable harvests and ski seasons, when large numbers of staff are required. These employment networks can only assist you once you have arrived.

Magazines

Specialist magazines can help you find overseas employment. I have listed some below. Under each work opportunity I have noted the names of those magazines which carry advertisements for that line of work.

International Job Finder is a monthly magazine published in the UK and distributed in several countries. It has a very helpful job section, along with feature articles on work opportunities abroad. It is available on subscription from:

International Job Finder

UK office	*Belgium*	Tel: (055) 314724
20–28 Dalling Road	*Denmark*	Tel: (45) 4632 7218
London W6 0JB	*France*	Tel: (01) 43 42 57 10
Tel: (020) 8237 8600		
Fax: (020) 8735 9942		

Overseas Jobs Express is a fortnightly newspaper published in the UK. It carries a variety of overseas positions and advertisements as well as information on work opportunities. It is available on a three-, six- or 12-month subscription. There is also a useful book store accessed via their website with books about working holidays, e.g. jobs on a cruise liner or work as a nanny. The website has an on-line job listing. Contact:

Overseas Jobs Express: www.overseasjobs.com
Premier House, Shoreham Airport
Sussex BN43 5FF, UK
Tel: (01273) 440220
Fax: (01273) 440229

Transitions Abroad is a bi-monthly US-produced publication. It does not advertise specific work opportunities but publishes a variety of articles on living, working, travelling and studying abroad. Every issue carries an extensive resource section. The magazine is available on subscription. Contact:

Transitions Abroad Publishing: www.transabroad.com
PO Box 3000
Amherst, MA 01004-1300, USA
Tel: (0413) 256 3414
Fax: (0413) 256 0373

Other magazines advertising overseas work opportunities include **specialist trade magazines**, such as those of official bodies and unions (teaching, accounting, nursing, hairdressing, etc.). Look for **specific magazines** covering positions in a single line of work, e.g. cruising, motorbikes (couriers), nannying or farming.

Also refer to the **employment sections of newspapers**. Most major newspapers are coming on-line now. There are also **backpacker magazines** in a number of countries. These are mentioned under the appropriate country in Chapter 7.

Travel brochures

Even though travel brochures are designed for travellers, they can be a good source of work information. They provide maps of specific areas (including popular tourist areas), mention tours available, details of special events and provide extensive lists of accommodation. You can use this available information to your advantage.

For instance, the accommodation will not only mention how many rooms are available but will mention what services the accommodation offers, like a beauty salon, tennis court, swimming pool, fitness centre, retail stores, coffee shop, restaurant, business centre, etc. You may like to approach them about a specific work opportunity. You will have the contact details in the travel brochure to do this.

Fellow travellers

Word of mouth from fellow travellers is a good way to find out about work opportunities. In many cases the travellers have experienced the type of work first-hand and can condone or condemn it.

SHOULD YOU ORGANISE WORK BEFORE YOU GO?

Organising work before you go depends on which visa you are entering a particular country with. For programs such as Au Pair and Camp America, your visa allows you to undertake work specific to that program and a job is organised before you go. A work visa is issued to those who are being transferred or contracted for a specific position. It is different for those of us going on working holidays.

Immigration officials can frown upon those who arrive on a working holiday visa with work pre-arranged. Even though you are allowed to find employment, pre-arranging it may go against your chances of being allowed into the country.

Remember most working holiday visas are issued on the premise that you are, firstly, going on a holiday and, secondly, taking only incidental work to fund further travels. Therefore, by pre-arranging work you are showing your intentions of working and this could be a breach of working holiday conditions.

There is no crime, however, if you contact the agencies in this guide for assistance and guidance on what work opportunities are available to you. In doing so, you are not breaching any work restrictions because these agencies cannot place you in a position until after you have arrived in the country.

A QUICK WORD ON TAX OBLIGATIONS

As mentioned in Chapter 2, you are required to apply for the appropriate tax number before you start work. If you do not obtain this number, your employer has no option but to deduct tax at a higher tax rate.

In some cases, half of your earnings can be taken in tax. Most employers will tax you under a PAYE (Pay As You Earn) scheme. Any tax taken out will be stipulated by the government legislation at the time. Your employer (or the tax office) will be able to advise you on the tax rates.

There may be other deductions taken from your salary such as a medical levy or superannuation (pension). If a superannuation amount is regularly deducted, you should find out if you are entitled to receive the total amount in cash when you finish working in the country, or whether it can be rolled over to another fund.

Some countries have double tax agreements where any money earned (including wages, commissions, bonuses, allowances, etc.) and any tax paid in another country may be required to be included on your tax return for your country of citizenship. As information on tax is rather complex and unique to individual countries, you may wish to make enquiries with the tax department in your country as to whether they have a double tax agreement with the country or countries you intend to work in.

Find out when the financial year ends. If you do not work a full year, or if you earned wages under the tax-free threshold (if the country has a tax-free threshold), then you may be entitled to a total or partial refund of the tax you have paid. Speak to your employer about this or the tax office of the overseas country you are working in. Companies which can help you obtain a tax refund advertise in backpacker magazines.

ABOUT THE EMPLOYMENT CONTACTS LISTED

The sections in this and the following chapters give an overview of what work is available and suggestions on how to find it. I suggest you contact the individual firms or employment agencies mentioned throughout this guide for the latest and most comprehensive information.

I have tried to cover as many work opportunities as possible. Of course, not every profession can be covered. Some of them are too specific, require your qualifications to be recognised, or involve sitting for qualifying tests—all too time-consuming and costly for a working holidaymaker, but hey, this gives you the perfect excuse to try something completely different—something that may truly give you a taste of another way of life or could turn into a new career.

Some of the employment agencies provide employment in a number of disciplines. I have therefore mentioned their full contact details under each discipline in which they appear. Note that all programs, employment agencies and other contacts listed in this guide are in alphabetical order and not in any order of preference of the author or publisher.

THE AUSTRALIA/NEW ZEALAND/ SOUTH AFRICA AND UNITED KINGDOM/ REPUBLIC OF IRELAND CONNECTION

For years now citizens of the United Kingdom and the Republic of Ireland have been heading to the southern hemisphere for working holidays while citizens from Australia, New Zealand and South Africa have been heading north for the same reason.

You will find there are many employment agencies with offices in Australia and the United Kingdom to capitalise on the large numbers of travellers who move between these countries. You will find a lot of these employment agencies mentioned in this travel guide.

If you are not from one of these countries and are on a working holiday, do not be worried about contacting these agencies. As long as you have the appropriate work visa and skills they are happy to help travellers find positions.

CHAPTER 6

Area Analysis

Positions mentioned under this section are expanded upon under the alphabetical work opportunity listing.

AFRICA

The general consensus by travellers is that travelling in Africa is extremely cheap. Many have found their finances have stretched much further than they ever imagined and they were able to live like 'kings and queens'. For this reason, and for the fact that living conditions are nowhere near as good as Western standards, many travellers have never even contemplated living and working in Africa. Can I say, 'Some countries are meant to be travelled in only, and Africa can be classified as one of them.'

It goes without saying that the countries on the African continent are very diverse. There are the Arab lands in the north and South Africa at the bottom. In between are countries (some impoverished) that have exquisite landscapes and vast deserts with unique cultures and wildlife.

At present, work opportunities in Africa are limited. For the purposes of this section I have divided Africa into three sections—Egypt and Morocco, South Africa and other African countries—mainly for my own convenience to describe the work available.

Egypt and **Morocco** are popular travel destinations. Those who seek work mostly find English teaching positions, particularly in Cairo and Alexandria (Egypt), and Casablanca and Marrakech (Morocco). These major centres have several language schools offering courses to learn English. You could contact a school before you arrive or wait until you get there. Berlitz, EF Education and International House are three large organisations with schools in these cities. See the 'Teaching' section in Chapter 7 for details. Some travellers place advertisements offering one-on-one English lessons.

Others find positions in the hospitality industry. Cairo, Alexandria, Casablanca and Marrakech have many hotels and bars. Many find a position by door-knocking or through hostel noticeboards.

Another way could be to pick up travel brochures. Here you will find a list of accommodation available which should mention the services they offer. These can include cafes, restaurants, beauty parlours, fitness centres, etc. You could then apply for a specific position, or a number of positions, directly to the accommodation site as you will have the contact details in the brochure.

With the large number of tourists visiting Egypt and Morocco, many tour companies require 'reps' to meet and greet incoming tour groups. You may wish to contact the companies which specialise in such tours. These include Contiki, Globus and Cosmos, Insight, Top Deck and Trafalgar Tours. Refer to Chapter 4.

Since the change in political climate, more travellers have been visiting **South Africa**. The country's policy is now to get its own citizens into employment. Unfortunately, this means there are limited positions available to travellers as in most cases the locals are quite prepared to accept a lower wage than most travellers. There are, however, positions still available, particularly in the bars, hostels and hotels in the major centres, such as Johannesburg and Durban.

The **other African countries** do not yield many work opportunities besides teaching and aid work. Agencies to contact include Amnesty International, Care International, Medecins Sans Frontiers, the Red Cross, the United Nations and World Vision. For details on aid agencies see 'Volunteer work and programs' in Chapter 7.

There are a number of companies (which a visit to a travel agent will reveal) offering tours through various countries in Africa, and they need cooks, campsite managers and drivers. Even though local tour guides are used, many tourists prefer a tour guide from their own country or one who speaks their language fluently. Contact the companies' head offices for positions available. You often need to have extensive knowledge of the area or areas and be able to cope with border crossings, vehicle breakdowns, the wildlife, etc. Some major tour companies include Acacia, Contiki, Dragoman Adventure Travel, Encounter Overland, Globus and Cosmos, Insight, Intrepid, Peregrine Adventure Travel, Top Deck, Trafalgar Tours and World Expeditions. You can find their office details by looking on their tour brochures, or refer to Chapter 4 for their website addresses.

AUSTRALIA

Australia has a **working holiday visa** available to citizens of Canada, the Republic of Ireland, Japan, the Republic of Korea, Malta, the Netherlands and the United Kingdom. This allows people from these countries to apply for a one-year working holiday in Australia.

Applicants should be single (although married couples without children are eligible), aged between 18 and 25 years 11 months.

If you are from a 'non-arrangement' country, or aged 26 to 30 years 11 months, you may still apply, but you are required to submit a statement explaining how a visit to Australia will be of benefit both to Australia and to yourself. Contact your nearest Australian Consulate, Embassy or High Commission for details.

Although many working holidaymakers travel to Australia off their own bat, there are support programs available through the Council on International Educational Exchange (Council) and International Exchange Programs (IEP). Basically, these organisations offer support before and during your time in Australia. For more details on these organisations refer to the section on 'Programs' in Chapter 5.

To work in Australia you must apply for a Tax File Number soon after your arrival. You can do this at the nearest Taxation Office. If you do not apply for this number to give to prospective employers, your wages will be taxed at the maximum rate.

Australia has several travel clubs which are good starting points; for a small joining fee they offer a variety of services such as: mail holding; luggage storage; all your travel needs including booking airfares, tours, etc., and travel insurance; links to budget accommodation; advice on finding work; noticeboards with a variety of information; and access to computers to type up your CV and surf the Internet. Travel clubs include:

Global Travel Team: www.globaltravelteam.com
Level 2, 88 Pitt Street
Sydney NSW 2000
Tel: (02) 9235 0231
Fax: (02) 9235 0379

International Travellers Advisory Service (ITAS):
www.itas.com.au
552 Crown Street
Surry Hills NSW 2010
Tel: (02) 9262 5011
Fax: (02) 9262 5551

Japanese visitors may wish to visit:
Australia–Japanese Working Holiday Office
10 Quay Street
Haymarket NSW 2000
Tel: (02) 9281 0090
Fax: (02) 9281 0158

Travellers Contact Point: www.travellers.com.au

Sydney
Level 7, 428 George Street
Tel: (02) 9221 8744
Fax: (02) 9221 3746

Melbourne
29–31 Somerset Place
Tel: (03) 9642 2911
Fax: (03) 9642 2944

Cairns
1st Floor, 13 Shields Street
Tel: (07) 4041 4677
Fax: (07) 4041 1338

Perth
499 Wellington Street
Tel: (08) 9226 0660
Fax: (08) 9226 0660

Darwin
11 Knucky Street
Tel: (08) 8941 0070
Fax: (08) 8981 3053

There are a few very useful backpacker magazines produced in Australia for working holiday travellers. The two most notable are *Aussie Backpacker* and *TNT Magazine Australia*.

Aussie Backpacker is a bi-monthly publication available free throughout Australia at most hostels, airports and train and coach terminals. It has loads of information for working holidaymakers to Australia including accommodation, work and travel options.

Published separately is an accommodation booklet about Australia which is filled with information regarding hostels. If you're not in Australia to pick up a copy, you can order over the Internet.
Aussie Backpacker: www.aussiebackpack.com.au
(published by the Australian Publishing Co. Pty Ltd):
440 Flinders Street
Townsville Qld 4810
Tel: (07) 4772 3244
Fax: (07) 4772 3250

TNT Magazine Australia provides very useful information for overseas visitors (particularly for those from the UK) on working holidays to Australia. There is information on work opportunities, accommodation and travel options.

It also contains up-to-date and important news from home, including football scores. There are four different editions, one for New South Wales (produced monthly), one for Queensland (monthly), one for the outback (bi-monthly), and one for Victoria and Tasmania (bi-monthly).

You can pick up a copy of the magazine free from various distribution points, including hostels, coach and train stations, airports and some travel agents.

TNT Magazine Australia: www.tntmag.com.au
Level 4, 46–48 York Street
Sydney NSW 2000
Tel: (02) 9299 4811
Fax: (02) 9299 4861

TNT Magazine Australia produces an *Independent Travellers' Guide to Australia & New Zealand*, available at Australian High Commissions in the United Kingdom or via the magazine's website.

There are also magazines aimed at office workers (which have advertisements for office-based positions) distributed in Sydney and Melbourne. These include *Nine to Five* (Sydney only) and *City Weekly* (both Sydney and Melbourne).

There are two sorts of working holidaymaker in Australia. There are those who set up home in Sydney, find employment and save to embark on their travels around Australia. Then there are those who pick up casual work as they travel around Australia.

Most working holidaymakers set up home in Sydney. They find a flat, a job and settle in to enjoy the Sydney summer, which includes spending Christmas Day partying on Bondi Beach. Then, as winter approaches, they head north to Queensland for the warmer weather.

Sydney has an abundance of work opportunities available, including office-based positions which are found through specialist employment agencies. Other possibilities include labouring work.

Many travellers find live-in au pair or nanny positions which takes care of finding accommodation and employment in one hit.

To nurse in Australia, you are required to obtain registration in the State you wish to nurse. This can be rolled over to other States. Once registration is obtained you can find a position through one of the many specialist nursing employment agencies.

There are hospitality positions available in bars and restaurants, particularly during the summer months (December to February).

There are many travellers, however, who like to get out of Sydney and experience other work opportunities. If you want to follow the sun there is year-round fruit and vegetable picking work available. There are hundreds of fruit and vegetable picking areas and there have been a number of books written on the subject. They not only have information on individual harvests but suggest accommodation, places to eat and visit and include many contact details. Harvest guides are also printed in the backpacker magazines.

If you want a taste of real Australian farm life then you could look for work on a farm or station as a jackaroo or jillaroo (Australian names for farm hands). If travelling along the Queensland coast, you may find a hospitality position on an island resort or as a deck hand or cook on a prawn trawler.

During the winter months (June to September) the ski season in New South Wales and Victoria is in full swing. Each March the call for employees is sent out to fill the positions available. If you missed this call, it can still be worth your while to arrive at the beginning of the season. It is suggested that you pick up travel brochures on the holiday resort (outback, Queensland coast or ski area) you wish to work. Here you will find a list of accommodation available. Each will mention the services they have to offer. Depending on the size of the establishment these can include cafes, restaurants, beauty parlours, fitness centres, swimming pools, tennis courts, ski hire, etc. You could then apply for a specific position, or a number of positions, directly to the accommodation as you will have its full contact details in the brochure.

For more information, contact details of employment agenices and suggestions on how to find office-based employment, childcare work, nursing agencies, farm jobs, fruit and vegetable picking and ski positions, see the appropriate sections in Chapter 7.

Other major cities—Adelaide, Brisbane, Cairns, Darwin, Melbourne, Perth—also offer various work opportunities to travellers.

There are many specialist employment agencies linking travellers with work opportunities. They can be found through the backpacker magazines and telephone books. Other travellers are also a good source of information, as are hostel noticeboards. Hostels may offer employment as receptionists, cleaners, kitchen staff and for those with their own mini-buses, drivers to pick up and drop off backpackers at train and coach stations. Travellers may wish to contact Employment National, the government-run employment agency. You can access the website which provides an insight into the Australian job market at: www.centrelink.gov.au

Australia has several English language schools to cater for the large number of overseas people who come to learn English. For those with the University of Cambridge/Royal Society of Arts Courses (Cambridge/RSA) Certificate or the Trinity Certificate in Teaching English from Trinity College, you have your choice of jobs. Refer to the 'Teaching' section in Chapter 7 for more details on schools.

More detailed information can be found in *Live, Work and Play in Australia*, published by Kangaroo Press.

CANADA

Canada has a one-year **working holiday visa** available to 18- to 25-year-old citizens of Australia, New Zealand, Japan, the United Kingdom, Ireland, Korea, Belgium and France.

A limited number of working holiday visas are issued each year from 2 January. Visas are issued until the allocated quota for that year is filled. Contact the nearest Canadian Consulate or High Commission for full details and an application form. Those intending to work in health, teaching and child care will be required to undergo and pass a medical examination. You should attach a note with your visa application, requesting medical instructions.

If your application is successful, a Letter of Introduction will be issued. This must be presented on your arrival in Canada to an immigration official who will issue your 'Employment Authorisation'. You cannot work in Canada without this authorisation. Canada has a special work agreement with the USA for US citizens.

On arrival, you are required to apply for a Social Insurance Number. You cannot get paid for work in Canada without a Social Insurance Number. Normally this can take up to six weeks.

Though many go to Canada off their own bat, if you are feeling a little daunted about travelling on your own, then you may consider contacting the Council on International Educational Exchange (Council) or International Exchange Programs (IEP) which offer support programs. For more details on these organisations refer to the section on 'Programs' in Chapter 5.

Students (or recent graduates) from Australia or New Zealand may be interested in the **Student Work Abroad Program (SWAP)**, which is exclusively run each year by STA. Places on the program are limited. Information brochures are released each April with 'swappers' leaving either independently up to October or in a group departure in late November and early December. The program assists you in travelling from your home to Vancouver, but from there to elsewhere in Canada, you're on your own.

SWAP does not place program participants directly into employment, but their team in Vancouver can help you in your search for work. The application fee for SWAP Canada includes: processing of your working holiday visa; one-way transfer from Vancouver Airport to downtown Vancouver; two nights' accommodation in a downtown YHA; a comprehensive orientation; a travel guide to Canada and pre-departure information kit; and ongoing assistance in Canada. You also get fast-track processing of your Social Insurance Number. Swappers who attend the orientation sessions will get their number processed in six working day, which, as previously mentioned, can take up to six weeks.

Australians and New Zealand citizens should contact their nearest STA Travel for more information and an application form. Working holidaymakers usually spend their time in the English-speaking provinces of British Columbia and Alberta on the west coast or Ontario on the east coast. Work in the French-speaking provinces can be limited for English-speakers, but it is not impossible to find.

Many set up shop in Vancouver in British Columbia or Toronto in Ontario, which offer travellers a variety of work opportunities including hospitality, secretarial and labouring jobs. Most find work through employment agencies or advertisements in newspapers like *Vancouver Sun* or *Toronto Sun*, and by knocking on doors.

Many females find jobs as nannies or au pairs with Canadian families. There are a number of specialist agencies which can help place you in this type of position.

The ski season runs from November/December to March/April, and provides a vast number of positions. You will be competing with thousands of other travellers coming to secure work. It is suggested you pick up travel brochures on skiing in Canada. The brochures are very informative as regards the ski resorts. These include the number of runs, the services available including ski hire, cafes, restaurants, etc., plus extensive lists of accommodation available. You could then use this information when seeking work as you will have the contact details in the brochures. For more information refer to the 'Ski centres' section in Chapter 7.

Fruit and vegetable picking is also available. Refer to Canada under 'Fruit and vegetable picking' in the 'Agriculture and Farming' section in Chapter 7.

Canada Employment Weekly is a weekly publication listing a variety of professional positions in a number of fields throughout Canada. It is available by subscription.

Canada Employment Weekly: www.mediacorp2.com
(published by Mediacorp Canada Inc.)
15 Madison Avenue
Toronto, Ontario M5R 2S2, Canada
Tel: (0416) 964 6069
Fax: (0416) 964 3202

THE CARIBBEAN

The Caribbean is made up of a number of islands, including Antigua, Barbados, Jamaica and Trinidad, to name a few. Some belong to other countries, including the UK, France and the Netherlands, so check if there are work-visa links available between these countries and your own.

The Panama Canal transformed the Caribbean Sea into the busiest shipping route in the western hemisphere. It is a short-cut between the Atlantic and Pacific oceans. Travellers therefore are able to hitch a ride or work a passage to other islands or on Atlantic crossings. The most popular time for sailing in the Caribbean is between September and April. To find work, try any harbour where seafaring vessels are anchored and speak to the captain, or place an advertisement on a yacht club's or sailing school's noticeboard. Refer to 'Yacht crewing' in Chapter 7 for more details.

The popularity of the Caribbean means many cruise liners sail this area. They usually begin their journey from Miami, Florida. You may wish to contact cruise lines and employment agencies in Miami for a position. Major cruise lines include Celebrity Cruise Lines, Carnival Cruise Lines, Festival Cruises, Royal Caribbean International and Princess Cruises. However most cruise lines do not employ staff themselves, preferring to find staff through concessionnaires. For more details see Chapter 7.

Some travellers find hospitality positions in the resorts on the islands. It is suggested you pick up travel brochures on the specific island you wish to work. Here you will find a list of resorts and other accommodation available. Each resort will mention the services they have to offer. These can include cafes, restaurants, beauty parlours, fitness centres, swimming pools, tennis courts, etc. You could then apply for a specific position, or a number of positions, directly to the resort as you will have its full contact details in the brochure.

CENTRAL AND SOUTH AMERICA

Unfortunately, there are no working holiday schemes available which allow people from overseas to work in any of the countries on the South American continent. Central and South America seem to be areas that are 'meant to be travelled'! There are, however, opportunities available.

Most find work teaching English through an English language school or on a one-to-one basis in the major cities. You can arrange a position beforehand or arrive and approach schools individually.

Those with the University of Cambridge/Royal Society of Arts Courses (Cambridge/RSA) Certificate or the Trinity Certificate in Teaching English from Trinity College do have an advantage to landing the best jobs. North Americans also have an advantage as South

America is geared towards the US lifestyle. But these things are not absolutely necessary to land a job. If you are accepted as a teacher, the school should help you change your visa status from holiday-maker to work permit. They may also help with accommodation or advise where to find something long-term.

To find work, have a look in the telephone books, on hostel noticeboards (or place your own ad), on university noticeboards (as students may wish to improve their English and thus their employment opportunities) and in the English-language papers such as *The News* in Mexico City, *The Daily Journal* in Venezuela and *El Mercurio* in Chile.

Large institutions including Berlitz, EF Education and International House have schools you may wish to approach. For more information on teaching English refer to 'Teaching English' in the 'Teaching' section in Chapter 7.

There are a number of specialist companies which require guides to lead their tours. Even though local tour guides are used, many travellers like the comfort of a guide from their own country or one who speaks their language fluently. Some major tour companies include Dragoman Adventure Travel, Encounter Overland, Globus and Cosmos, Intrepid, Peregrine Adventure Travel and World Expeditions. You can find their office details by looking on their tour brochures or, refer to Chapter 4 for their website addresses.

In leading holiday destinations (such as Cancun and Acapulco in Mexico and Rio de Janeiro in Brazil) that are particularly frequented by Americans, you may find a position working in a hotel or bar. It is suggested you pick up travel brochures on the specific area you wish to work. Here you will find a list of the resorts and other accommodation available. Each resort will mention the services they have to offer. These can include cafes, restaurants, beauty parlours, fitness centres, swimming pools, tennis courts, etc. You could then apply for a specific position, or a number of positions, directly to the resort as you will have its full contact details in the brochure.

You may also wish to contact an aid agency. These include Amnesty International, Care International, Medecins Sans Frontiers, the Red Cross, the United Nations and World Vision. More details on these aid agencies are included under 'Volunteer work and programs' in Chapter 7.

As many areas have uncovered ancient civilisations there may be opportunities to volunteer on an archaeological dig. Details of organisations which oversee digs are mentioned under 'Archaeological digs' in the 'Volunteer work and programs' section in Chapter 7.

EASTERN EUROPE AND THE COMMONWEALTH OF INDEPENDENT STATES

The more favourable political climate of Eastern Europe and the Commonwealth of Independent States (CIS) sees more travellers not only visiting these areas but securing positions.

The variety of positions is limited, so most travellers find hospitality positions in a tourist area, work as a tour guide or coach driver for a tour company, apply for an aid-worker position or approach an English language school to teach English.

EUROPEAN UNION AND EUROPEAN ECONOMIC AREA

After the devastation of World War II, several European countries sought ways to make sure that they would never go to war against each other again. It was therefore decided that countries would join forces to achieve mutual benefit and lasting peace. That idea has today become the European Union (EU) and currently consists of 15 countries (known as member states): Austria, Belgium, Denmark, Finland, France, Germany, Greece, the Republic of Ireland, Italy, Luxembourg, the Netherlands, Portugal, Spain, Sweden and the United Kingdom.

It should be noted that citizens of member states are now citizens of the EU. This does not effect any individual's nationality, culture or language.

Mutual benefit is being achieved in a number of ways. For extensive information on this, contact your nearest European Commission office or have a look at their website: www.europa.eu.int

Basically, restrictions have been lifted on the movement of goods, services, capital and people between all member states. This has created several benefits: qualifications gained in one member state are recognised in another, giving citizens access to more job opportunities with terms and conditions of employment the same anywhere in the EU; travel between member states is made easier and quicker with the easing of restrictions at Customs control points; and if citizens become ill in another member state, they have access to that member state's health services via reciprocal health agreements.

Iceland and Norway have not joined the European Union but are part of the European Economic Area (EEA) and citizens from these countries can live and work in EU member countries just as EU members can live and work in EEA countries.

There are many employment opportunities for citizens of member states in other member states in both the EU and EEA. However, there may be language barriers to overcome, particularly in positions which require contact with the public.

One of the strategies of the EU has been to introduce EURES (European Public Employment Service). This is the public employment service of the EU and the EEA. Citizens of EU and EEA member states can access EURES for advice on job opportunities and living and working conditions of other EU and EEA countries. There are around 500 Euroadvisors (offices) in the countries. You are able to search job vacancies in particular countries, for example, office clerks in Ireland, construction positions in Greece, catering positions in Spain. You can also do more localised searches via individual country's jobcentres. You can also do this via their websites. It should be noted that not all of them are in English:

Austria: Arbeitsmarktservice (AMS): www.ams.or.at
Belgium: ORBEM (for Brussells area): www.orbem.be
Denmark: Arbeidsformidlingen (AMS): www.af.dk (gen info) *or* www.eures.dk (EURES info)
Finland: ML: www.mol.fi
France: l'Agence Nationale Pour l'Emploi (ANPE): www.anpe.fr
Germany: Bundesverwaltungsamt (BVA): www.auslandsschulwesen.de
Greece: OAED: www.oaed.gr
Iceland: Vinnumalastofnun: www.vinnumalastofnun.is
Ireland: Foras Aiseanna Saothair (FAS): www.fas.ie
Italy: AML: www.europalavoro.it
Luxembourg: Administration de l'Emploi (ADEM): www.etat.lu
Netherlands: Arbeidsbureau (AV): www.arbeidsbureau.nl
Norway: Arbeidsmarkedsetaten: www.aetat.no
Portugal: Instituto do Emprego E Formacao Profissional (IEFP): www.iefp.pt
Spain: INEM: www.inem.es
Sweden: Arbetsformedlingen (AMS): www.amv.se
UK: Employment Service: www.employmentservice.gov.uk

The introduction of the Euro, the single unit of currency, on 1 January 1999 in 11 member states, has created many banking, financial and IT jobs. You may need to be bilingual to secure such work.

There are many casual and seasonal work opportunities available. Many of these are found in the fruit and vegetable picking areas; in ski resorts during the ski season; and at beach clubs and on yachts and charter boats in the Mediterranean and the Aegean Sea during the summer months. Refer to these sections in Chapter 7. Unfortunately, due to language barriers, many travellers are allocated to menial jobs such as dish washing, cleaning or being a busboy.

Au pair and nanny positions can be found with families throughout the EU and EEA. You will find that many EU and EEA families are more open-minded about having a male child-minder. There are numerous au pair and nanny agencies able to help find positions. *The Lady* magazine (details under 'United Kingdom' in the 'Nanny, mother's help and au pair positions' section in Chapter 7) is a very helpful publication to obtain as it carries advertising from not only specialist employment agencies offering child-care positions but families who advertise directly in the publication.

For non-EU passport holders, work is much harder to find.

Those with a University of Cambridge/Royal Society of Arts Courses (Cambridge/RSA) Certificate or the Trinity Certificate in Teaching English from Trinity College obtain the best positions. If you are accepted as a teacher, the school should help you change your visa status from holidaymaker to work permit. They may also help with accommodation or advise where to find something long-term. Large institutions including Berlitz, EF Education and International House have schools in these countries. Refer to 'Teaching English' in the 'Teaching' section in Chapter 7. There are smaller privately owned schools offering positions. Look in telephone books, on hostel noticeboards (or place your own advertisement) and on university noticeboards (as students may wish to improve their English and their employment opportunities). Some travellers offer one-on-one tuition. You may consider offering this in return for room and board.

Some travellers find positions with the tour companies (particularly the 18 to 30-something tours) as coach drivers, tour guides and as reps at sites throughout Europe. Contact them for opportunities.

The Netherlands has a **working holiday scheme** with Australia, Canada and New Zealand. If you are under the age of 26, you may be interested in this visa.

On arrival, and before you can begin work, you are required to register with the local police and obtain a tax file number and work permit (both of these can take about two months to be processed).

Traditionally, travellers have found positions in the flower-bulb industry where they are required to either dig the bulbs up or peel and sort the bulbs for packing. The bulb season runs during the summer months from mid-June to September.

Positions can be found in the hospitality industry particularly in bars in Amsterdam. There are a number of hostels here which often take travellers to work as reception staff or as cleaners and maintenance staff. Those with child-care experience may wish to secure a live-in au pair position.

REPUBLIC OF IRELAND

The Republic of Ireland is a member state of the European Union, therefore citizens of other member states can go to the Republic to live, work and play.

The Republic of Ireland has a **working holiday visa** available to citizens from Australia and New Zealand. This allows those aged between 18 and 25 a one-year stay.

Authorities will tell you that Ireland has a high unemployment rate so your chances of finding work are slim. But many still do.

Most working holidaymakers set up home in Dublin where there are many employment opportunities, including jobs in the hospitality industry (especially bartending), nannying and office work. Those with an EU passport could also get in touch with Foras Aiseanna Saothair (FAS), which is the Irish employment service. You can access the FAS website at www.fas.ie

This site allows you to do a search for available jobs. You can also localise this job search. For example, look for catering work in a southern county. There are also private employment agencies you could register with to help you find work.

Pick up some travel brochures on Ireland. Here you will find a list of accommodation available which should mention the services they have to offer. These can include cafes, restaurants, beauty parlours, fitness centres, golf courses, etc. You could then apply for a specific position, or a number of positions directly to the accommodation as you will have its full contact details in the brochure.

The cultural centre of Dublin is the Temple Bar area, located on the southern bank of the River Liffey. Here there is an abundance of bars, cafes, restaurants and boutiques where positions can be found mostly by door-knocking.

Hospitality positions can be found around the Republic in the major holiday centres, for example Limerick and Cork.

Delphi Adventure Holidays is located in south-west Mayo on the west coast and provides year-round adventure and education courses. It requires qualified instructors to lead activities such as sailing, kayaking, windsurfing, canoeing, abseiling, rock climbing, archery, badminton, tennis, waterskiing, etc., and catering staff. For details refer to the 'Holiday camps' section in Chapter 7. Some travellers find positions as catering assistants or as instructors at holiday camps.

ISRAEL

Most travellers to Israel seeking work join a kibbutz or a moshav as a volunteer.

VOLUNTEERING ON A KIBBUTZ

A kibbutz is a communal settlement where everything earned and produced is shared by all kibbutz members. Kibbutzim (plural of kibbutz) provide travellers with the opportunity to live and work as part of these communal settlements by taking on volunteers. Traditionally, positions were of an agricultural type, but some kibbutzim have diversified to offer services in manufacturing and tourism.

Travellers can join a kibbutz as a volunteer for a minimum of two months and a maximum of six months. The working hours and work required will vary according to the kibbutz you are assigned to. In general, you will be required to work eight hours a day, six days a week. Your day will start early (probably at 6am), which will mean an early finish, giving you time to do things in the afternoon. You will be expected to do the job assigned to you which could be picking fruit, milking cows, washing dishes, etc. This work can be tedious and boring and undertaken in extreme heat.

In exchange for work, you receive accommodation (which is basic and will be shared with up to four other volunteers per room), meals, work clothes (including shoes) and pocket money. Volunteers are usually taken on day trips once a month. The number of day trips can increase the longer you stay. You will also have access to the kibbutz facilities, including tennis courts and swimming pools.

There are two ways to find positions on a kibbutz: through a kibbutz office in Tel Aviv or through a representative in another country which can organise a position before you arrive. It can be much cheaper to organise a position once you are in Israel as the kibbutz representative companies can charge a hefty fee for placement. However, if you arrive in Israel to arrange a position, be aware that you are not guaranteed one immediately. You may have to wait a few days or weeks before a placement is found. Therefore, you will have to support yourself during this initial period.

Kibbutz Program Centre
18 Frishman Street
Tel Aviv 65134, Israel
Tel: (03) 527 8874
Fax: (03) 523 9966

The office is open from Sunday to Thursday 8am to 2pm. Take your passport, medical certificate (it has recently been introduced that volunteers must undergo an HIV test before placement), insurance policy, airline ticket, registration fee and two passport photos.

The Kibbutz Program Centre has a very useful website with extensive information including 'what is a kibbutz?' and 'how to become a volunteer'. There is a listing of kibbutz program desks around the world which you can contact for information or to organise a position before you arrive (some are listed below). Also included is a 'volunteers' forum' where you can read first-hand experiences of travellers who have volunteered on a kibbutz.

There are Kibbutz Program Centre desks in representative offices in continental Europe (the Netherlands, Spain, Austria, Germany, France, Italy, Denmark, Finland, Hungary, Sweden and Poland) and Asia (Japan, Turkey, Korea and Russia). Look at www.kibbutz.org.il for full contact details. Some offices are:

Kibbutz Program Centre

Australia
Sydney:
146 Darlinghurst Road
Sydney NSW 2010
Tel: (02) 9360 6300

Melbourne:
308 Hawthorn Road
Caulfield Vic 3162
Tel: (03) 9272 5531

France
Objectif Kibbutz
37 Blvd Magenta
Paris 75010
Tel: (01) 4203 4290
Fax: (01) 4206 1140

Holland
Oppenheim Travel
Cronenburg 154
1081 GN Amsterdam
Tel: (020) 404 2040
Fax: (020) 404 4055

Japan
Temasa Travel
2 342 2 Denenchofu
Ota-ku, Tokyo 145
Tel: (03) 3722 2184
Fax: (03) 3722 4421

North America
110 East 59th Street
New York NY 10022, USA
Tel: (0212) 318 6130

New Zealand
Auckland:
528 Parnell Road
Auckland
Tel: (09) 309 9444

Wellington:
Wellington Zionist Society
PB27156, Wellington
Tel/Fax: (04) 384 4229

Russia
Jewish Agency
Moscow
Tel: (095) 253 8320
Fax: (095) 253 4667

United Kingdom
1a Accommodation Road
London NW11 8ED
Tel: (020) 8458 9235

South Africa
OVC Johannesburg
The Colony Centre
Cr Jan Smuts & Rothesay Avenue
Craighall Park
Tel: (011) 880 3635

Kibbutz Adventure Centre
For kibbutz and moshav positions: www.kibbutz.com.au

Australia
Level 23, Tower 1
500 Oxford Street
Bondi Junction NSW 2022
Tel: (02) 9513 8875
Fax: (02) 9513 8879

Israel
66 Ben Yehuda Street
Tel Aviv 63432
Tel/Fax: (03) 524 7973

Project 67
10 Hatton Gardens
London EC1N 8AH, UK
Tel: (020) 7831 7626

VOLUNTEERING ON A MOSHAV
A moshav is an alternative to working on a kibbutz. A kibbutz works as a collective and you work for the kibbutz, while on a moshav, you work for a family. Each family has its own fields and equipment (machinery, tractors, etc.).

Work is generally harder on a moshav and the family will advise you as to what will be required during your working hours. You will be working eight hours a day, six days week—and during high seasons maybe longer, for which you will receive paid overtime.

The family provides separate accommodation, which will be basic but have bathroom and kitchen facilities. Sometimes you will join the family for meals but usually you will be expected to prepare your own meals.

You can organise a position on a moshav from:

Moshav Movement
19 Leonardo Da Vinci Street
Tel Aviv 65134, Israel

Israel does offer travellers some other work opportunities, including many jobs in bars, restaurants, travellers' hostels and hotels, particularly in the main cities of Tel Aviv and Jerusalem. Many find a position by door-knocking or through hostel noticeboards. Another way could be to pick up travel brochures. Here you will find a list of accommodation available which should mention the services they offer. These can include cafes, restaurants, beauty parlours, fitness centres, etc. You could then apply for a specific position, or a number of positions, directly to the accommodation site as you will have its full contact details in the brochure.

As mentioned on the Kibbutz website, construction work is available in Eilat, which is by the Red Sea. Apparently Eilat is a 'boom town' and many construction managers needing workers drive past the Peace Cafe at 6am and collect staff for the day.

There are a number of English language schools which may require teachers of English. Contact them directly. The best positions are usually offered to those with the University of Cambridge/Royal Society of Arts Courses (Cambridge/RSA) Certificate or the Trinity Certificate in Teaching English from Trinity College.

Some travellers find positions as au pairs or secretaries. Look in the papers such as the English-language *Jerusalem Post* which carries advertisements. Also contact major employment agencies such as Manpower.

As large numbers of tourists visit Israel, there are a number of tour companies who require 'reps' to meet and greet incoming tour groups. Other companies may require tour leaders and bus drivers. Some major tour companies include Acacia, Contiki, Dragoman Adventure Travel, Encounter Overland, Globus and Cosmos, Insight, Intrepid, Peregrine Adventure Travel, Top Deck, Trafalgar Tours and World Expeditions. You can find their office details by looking on their tour brochures or refer to Chapter 4.

Though most associate Israel with hot weather and desert or beach terrain, you may find work in the Mount Hermon ski field.

If you are interested in volunteering to work on an archaeology site, then you may have the opportunity while in Israel. The Israel Antiquities Authorities oversees the excavations so contact them in Jerusalem (Tel: (02) 292607). Some digs are also mentioned on hostel noticeboards. For more information on digs refer to 'Archaeological digs' in the 'Volunteer work and programs' section in Chapter 7.

JAPAN

Some travellers dismiss Japan as a working holiday destination for two reasons: 1) they believe it is extremely expensive; and 2) they don't speak Japanese.

First, yes, Japan can be expensive, you will find a piece of fruit or a cup of coffee selling for 100 times what it would be at home.

Therefore, you need to learn to live (including eat) like the locals as soon as possible. Keep in mind that there is a large ex-pat scene in Japan, and your fellow travellers will be able to advise you on how to survive as cheaply as possible.

Secondly, not speaking the language is not necessarily a problem. Many new arrivals cannot speak a word of Japanese, but they immerse themselves in the culture and learn the language that way. If you are worried about not speaking Japanese, then do a course before you go.

Japan has a **working holiday visa** available to citizens from Australia, New Zealand, Canada and Korea aged between 18 and 30. The working holiday visa is available for a stay of up to six months. It allows you to take work for up to 20 hours per week, and can be extended twice, giving you a maximum total stay of 18 months. The visa is a single-entry one so you must obtain a re-entry permit before leaving Japan. Contact your nearest Japanese Consulate for information and an application form.

There are many opportunities to teach English on contract. Several companies advertise outside of Japan for teachers. By going to Japan through one of these organisations, you will be offered a contract, usually for one year, and will enter with a work permit allowing you to take full-time work. Many British, Americans, Australians and New Zealanders enter Japan on a work permit. Details can be found under 'Teaching English in Japan' in the 'Teaching' section in Chapter 7.

The **Japan Exchange and Teaching (JET) Program** began in 1987 and is coordinated by the Council of Local Authorities for International Relations (CLAIR). There are three levels under the JET Program at which participants can enter Japan. These are: Assistant Language Teachers (ALT), who must have a degree to teach in schools; Coordinators for International Relations (CIR), who are placed in administration positions; and Sports Exchange Advisers (SEA), who promote international exchange through sports training.

All contracts are for one year. Applications close in December of each year with participants arriving in Japan in July each year. Participants must apply to the JET office in their home country (including Australia, Canada, Ireland, New Zealand, the United Kingdom and the USA) through the nearest Japanese High Commission or Consulate. If successful, your visa, job placement, accommodation, etc., will be arranged for you.

When staying longer than 90 days in Japan you must register as an 'alien' at the city issuing office nearest to where you are living.

Work out where you will be living first. Then within the 90 days take your passport and two passport-size photos to the city hall, city office or town office to register. Be prepared to spend the day at the issuing office for this registration. You will receive a temporary Alien Card on the spot, and then you will need to return to that office within a few weeks to pick up your actual Alien Card which you must carry with you at all times.

A good starting point may be one of the offices of the **Japan Association for Working Holiday Makers (JAWHM)**. These have been set up by the Japanese Ministry of Labour to help working holidaymakers. Here, you can obtain advice on the Japanese lifestyle, travel, employment and accommodation. You will need to register with JAWHM to use its services. There are two offices:

Tokyo
7th Floor, Sunplaza
4-1-1 Nakano
Nakano-ku, Tokyo 164-0001
(nearest train station:
Nakano on the JR Chuo line)
Tel: (03) 3389 0181
Fax: (03) 3389 1563

Osaka
2nd Floor, 2-3-1 Miharadai
Sakai City Osaka 590-0111
(nearest train station: Izumigaoka on the Senboku-Kousoku line)
Tel: (0722) 96 5741
Fax: (0722) 96 5752

Most *gaijin* (foreigners) in Japan find work teaching English. There are two ways for finding such work. First, a job can be arranged for you before you go by one of the companies that recruit outside Japan. Aeon and Nova are two such corporations. Their details can be found under 'Teaching English in Japan' in Chapter 7.

Others arrive in Japan and begin the search. Positions are widely advertised in Tokyo's Monday edition of the *Japan Times* and the monthly English magazine *Kansai Time Out* if in Osaka and Kyoto. Other *gaijin* are also a good source.

Work opportunities also arise in the hospitality industry, particularly in tourist hotels, *onsen* resorts (hot-spring resorts) and ski resorts during the ski season, which runs between December and April. If you wish to try your luck for work in these resorts it is suggested you pick up travel brochures on the specific area you wish to work. Here you will find a list of the resorts (sometimes with maps showing where each area is) which will mention the services they have to offer. These can include cafes, restaurants, beauty parlours, fitness centres, swimming pools, tennis courts, ski hire, etc. You could then apply for a specific position, or a number of positions, directly to the resort as you will have its full contact details in the brochure. People with excellent Japanese-language skills may find positions as translators or proofreaders with English magazines and newspapers, advertising agencies and marketing companies.

Hostesses (and hosts) are sought for positions in bars where they are required to entertain the customers, usually businessmen. This can be as simple as talking to them, pouring their drinks, lighting their cigarettes, etc. These positions are often found by door-knocking, through hostel noticeboards and via fellow *gaijin* already working at this. It should be noted that prostitution is illegal in Japan and these hostess (host) positions are not meant to be in this category.

THE MEDITERRANEAN

During the northern hemisphere summer, the Mediterranean becomes a popular playground for the rich, the famous and anyone else who wants to holiday in this sun-drenched area.

The Mediterranean region is large and encompasses a number of distinct areas, including the Spanish coast (including the Costa del Sol and the Balearic Islands of Majorca, Minora and Ibiza), the French coast (the Riviera, including Monte Carlo), the Italian coast, the Greek coast (including the Greek Islands) and the coast along the African continent. Many seeking work find bar and restaurant positions in these popular playgrounds. Others find work on one of the many boats cruising the area.

Malta has a one-year **working holiday visa** available to Australians and New Zealanders aged between 18 and 25. The island could be used as a base for travel in the Mediterranean.

Work is limited and your chances of finding work may be hindered by not speaking Maltese. However, Malta is becoming a popular tourist centre and work could be found in bars or restaurants during the northern hemisphere summer when many tourists visit Malta. Positions could be found by door-knocking or picking up travel brochures. Here you will find a list of accommodations which should mention the services they offer, i.e. cafes, restaurants, beauty parlours, fitness centres, etc. You could then apply for a specific position, or a number of positions, directly to the accommodation site as you will have the contact details in the brochure. There may also be positions teaching English. You should contact schools directly.

THE MIDDLE EAST

To understand why there are specific work opportunities available in the Middle East you need to go back to the 1970s when the price of oil shot up to US$25 a barrel. After this happened, oil-producing countries in the Middle East (Saudi Arabia, Kuwait, United Arab Emirates, Qatar, Oman, Yemen) decided to use their new-found wealth to improve the standard of living of their peoples. Thus, they embarked upon programs to bring the infrastructure of this area out of its nomadic, tribal 17th-century existence into the 20th century.

With so much money available, it was decided that only the best would do, and to achieve the best, they would use only staff with specialist skills. At the time, staff with such skills could only be found outside of the Middle East. Thus, Westerners (British, Americans, Australians, New Zealanders, etc.) with the required skills were put on contracts to build schools, universities and hospitals. Money was no object in the construction, so many buildings are built like five-star hotels. Once the schools, universities and hospitals were built, staff were required as teachers, medical and nursing staff.

As time passes and Middle Eastern people are obtaining the necessary skills to perform the positions Westerners have held, positions for Westerners have diminished, but not extinguished, so there are still contracts available to live and work in the Middle East.

There are many advantages to working in the Middle East. There is the lure of big wages which are tax-free. You will also have your airfare provided, annual leave of between six and eight weeks, a bonus on completion of your contract, which is for one year (and renewable), and all health care and accommodation provided for free.

Now the Middle East isn't everyone's cup of tea. Despite the advantages mentioned, one major disadvantage can be the cultural differences between the Middle East and the West. As the Middle East governments are aware of such cultural differences, they have provided compounds where Westerners can freely live their own Western way of life with other Westerners.

You must obey some restrictions outside the compounds, e.g. not consuming any alcohol whatsoever. Also, females must adhere to a strict dress code. On leaving the Western compounds you must wear the *abaye*, which covers you from your shoulders to your ankles.

Also, no single people are allowed to go out on their own. If you do, you will attract attention and probably be questioned by the authorities. It's best to go out in groups.

Anyone taking a contract to work in the Middle East should go there with a very open mind and be prepared to accept the Middle Eastern way of life (which is what living, working and playing in another country is all about). If you feel you couldn't adapt to the culture of the Middle East because of the above restrictions, then *don't* go in the first place.

On your arrival in the Middle East the authorities will take your passport and issue you with an *ekama*, which gives you residency and will allow you to travel freely throughout the area. On completion of your contract, your passport will be returned to you. If you go on holidays outside of the Middle East, your passport will be returned to you also.

Most positions in the Middle East are for engineers, medical secretaries, teachers and allied health staff, including nurses. Most nurses who go to the Middle East are female as male nurses are only allowed to treat male patients but female nurses can treat both male and female patients. Refer to the appropriate sections in Chapter 7. There are a number of employment agencies who specialise in placing people in the Middle East. Refer to the 'Allied health' and 'Technical, industrial, trades and general labouring' sections. Also look in your industry magazines where some agencies advertise.

If you are interested in volunteering to work on an archaeology dig such as in Jordan, then there are opportunities to do so. For more information on digs refer to 'Archaeological digs' in the 'Volunteer work and programs' section in Chapter 7.

NEW ZEALAND

New Zealand has a **working holiday scheme** with Canada, Japan and the United Kingdom. If you are a citizen of these countries and aged between 18 and 30, you can apply for a 12-month working holiday visa. Australian citizens do not need a work permit for New Zealand as a special agreement exists between the two countries.

To work in New Zealand you are required to obtain an IRD Number which you apply for at the Inland Revenue. Without this number you will be taxed heavily. A good starting point for a working holiday in New Zealand could be at:

Travellers Contact Point
38 Fort Street
Auckland, New Zealand
Tel: (09) 300 7197
Fax: (09) 300 7198

TNT Magazine New Zealand is useful for people holidaying in New Zealand (including those on working holidays). There is information on work opportunities, accommodation and travel options. You can pick up a copy of this bi-monthly publication free from various distribution points, including hostels, coach and train stations, airports and some travel agents.

Working holidaymakers often set up home in one of the major cities—Auckland, Wellington or Christchurch—where there are numerous work opportunities and many employment agencies to help find positions. Most find work in the hospitality industry, in information technology, secretarial fields and labouring.

The ski season, which runs from June to September, is a major attraction for visitors to New Zealand, and employment can be found in the major ski areas. Refer to the 'Ski centres' section in Chapter 7.

New Zealand is very popular with the cruising community. Many yachties stop off there on their way to and from Australia and/or Panama. If looking for a 'lift', try the Auckland Harbour area. Work in dry docks may also be available.

SOUTH-EAST ASIA AND CHINA

The countries in the Asian region are very diverse. As with Africa, travelling in them can be extremely cheap which is why many prefer to travel, rather than work. However, if you wish to supplement your funds there are possibilities.

Apart from aid work through aid organisations including Amnesty International, Care International, the Red Cross, the United Nations and World Vision, or a position as a tour guide or driver with a specialist tour company such as Dragoman Adventure Travel, Encounter Overland, Intrepid or World Expeditions (where you will need extensive knowledge of the area and possibly speak some of the language), most travellers find work teaching English.

Having a University of Cambridge/Royal Society of Arts Courses (Cambridge/RSA) Certificate or the Trinity Certificate in Teaching English from Trinity College or degree to teach English will see you obtain the best positions with private English language schools. Some travellers arrange a position before they arrive or else they approach schools when they get there. If you are accepted as a teacher the school should help you change your visa status from holiday-maker to work permit. They may also help with accommodation or advise where to find something long-term.

Large institutions including Berlitz, EF Education and International House have schools you may wish to approach. There are small privately owned schools which can offer positions also. Have a look in the telephone books, on hostel noticeboards (or place your own ad), on university noticeboards (as students may wish to improve their English and thus their employment opportunities), and in the English-language newspapers, including: *The China Daily* (China); *Asian Wall Street Journal*, *The Hong Kong Standard*, *International*

Herald Tribune, South China Morning Post (Hong Kong; a good source for jobs, particularly on Saturday); *The Bali Post, The Jakarta Post* (Indonesia); *Malay Mail, New Straits Times, The Star* (Malaysia); *Business Times* (Singapore); *Bangkok Post* (Thailand).

Another option, particularly in remote areas where there may be no schools, may be to offer one-on-one English conversation lessons in return for a family home stay.

The Council on International Educational Exchange runs a program called Teach in China. The Council's contact details are in Chapter 5.

As Asia is a popular destination for many Westerners there may be the possibility of finding bar work or other hospitality positions in the major tourist meccas.

Some female travellers have taken positions as hostesses. There are different levels of hostessing and you should make certain you fully understand what is involved before accepting a position. Some places only require you to flirt with drinkers, who are usually businessmen, while others may require you to wear revealing attire such as a G-string or to be topless. Such hostessing work is often advertised on hostel noticeboards, or can be found by door-knocking or through friends. Friends, in fact, should be the ones to advise you on how reputable the individual clubs are.

Some travellers have fallen in love with Asia and decided to undertake full-time study (or have married), which allows them to stay. A prime example of this is in Bali where many Australians have opened Australian-style eateries and bars to cater for the large numbers of Australians and other tourists who visit each year.

The **Republic of Korea** has a **working holiday visa** available to citizens of Australia, Canada and Japan aged between 18 and 25 (and in some cases up to 30). This visa may be extended to include citizens of New Zealand. Contact your nearest Korean Consulate or Embassy for information and an application form. On your arrival in the Republic of Korea you have three months to register as an alien.

UNITED KINGDOM

The United Kingdom (UK) consists of the countries England, Scotland, Wales and Northern Ireland. The UK is a member state of the European Union (EU), which means that members of other EU countries are able to live and work freely in the UK.

For citizens of Commonwealth countries there are a number of visas available. If you are aged 17 to 27 inclusive, you can apply for the **working holiday visa** which entitles you to a two-year stay, during which time you can take incidental work to your holiday. If you have grandparents you can apply for the **UK Ancestry Visa** which allows you a stay of up to four years and allows you to take full-time work. If you have a UK parent you can apply for the **Right of Abode** or a UK passport. For full details regarding visas and passports, contact your nearest British Consulate-General. You can download information and application forms from the Internet. It is a mandatory requirement to have the appropriate visa stamped in your passport *before* you arrive in the UK.

Though many travel to the UK off their own bat, there are support programs available through Council and IEP. Refer to their details in Chapter 5 under 'Programs'.

For years Australians, New Zealanders, Canadians and other members of the Commonwealth, including South Africans and Zimbabweans, have been heading to the UK on working holidays. They usually head to London, where there are many work opportunities for those with the appropriate visa and skills.

If you are planning to work in the UK, the first thing to do is apply for a National Insurance Number from the Department of Social Security. You need this to be taxed correctly and to receive medical treatment under the National Health Service.

There are two types of working holidaymaker to the UK. The majority set up home in London, which they use as a base to live and work in and which to travel from. Then there are those who undertake a number of positions as they travel the country.

There is a routine that many working holidaymakers to the UK seem to adopt. They spend the winter months working, then from March/April they begin leaving on their jaunts through Europe taking in the Running of the Bulls and finishing at the Oktoberfest in Munich in September. They then return to the UK where they find somewhere to live and work, and then settle in for the winter again.

Work is available constantly throughout the year, though during the summer months when the UK is invaded by tourists, hospitality positions increase in number. This is also the time when many British take their holidays, creating many temporary and contract office-based positions.

Most working holidaymakers find positions in London where there are employment agencies able to place you in accounting and banking, office support, labouring, engineering, nursing and allied health, teaching, agriculture and nannying positions. Many agencies have offices or associations with other agencies in Australia, New Zealand and South Africa where you can gain information and register for work before you arrive. Some of these are mentioned in Chapter 7 under the appropriate work opportunity. Once in London, the easiest way to find the specialist employment agencies is to look for their advertisements in the free magazines *Nine to Five*, *Ms London*, *Girl About Town* and *Midweek*, which are given out at Tube stations, and the free backpacker magazines (see next page).

For those wishing to experience life in other areas of the UK, seasonal work is available, including hospitality positions in popular tourist areas such as the Lake District and Cornwall.

Many of these positions can be found by door-knocking or from advertisements in the free backpacker magazines. It is suggested that you pick up travel brochures on the specific area you wish to work. Here you will find a list of accommodation available.

Each will mention the services they have to offer. Depending on the size of the establishment these can include cafes, restaurants, beauty parlours, fitness centres, swimming pools, tennis courts, etc. You could then apply for a specific position, or a number of positions, directly to the accommodation as you will have its full contact details in the brochure. Hospitality positions can also be found in the ski fields of Scotland. There are five centres: Glencoe, the Nevis Range, in the Cairngorms, The Lecht and Glenshee. For more information refer to the 'Ski centres' section in Chapter 7.

The UK has many archaeological digs going on, so if you would like to volunteer to work on a site you could contact the Council of British Archaeology. Details can be found under 'Archaeological digs' in the 'Volunteer work and programs' section in Chapter 7.

For those interested in working with children, try contacting PGL Adventure who require group leaders and activity instructors including those with sailing, kayaking, windsurfing, canoeing, abseiling, rock climbing, archery, badminton, tennis, waterskiing, etc., skills. For details see the 'Holiday camps' section in Chapter 7.

The UK is an extremely popular destination for travellers. By reading about the travel options in the Travel chapter you will see just how many travel options there are.

Many of the companies who provide such options have geared their services to the 18 to 30-something market. Therefore, they employ many travellers who have undertaken their trips and understand what 'newcomers' require and want out of their tours.

Have a look at the travel options in Chapter 4, where you will find the names and contact details of such companies. While having a look at the websites of the tour companies mentioned, I found a number of them had information on employment opportunities with

their tour company. These included bus drivers and tour leaders for organised tours and jo-jos. ***TNT Magazine*** began in the UK in the 1980s. It provides extensive information (employment, accommodation and travel options) to Australians, New Zealanders and South Africans in the UK on working holidays. It reports up-to-date and important news from home, including rugby, Australian Rules and cricket scores. It is a weekly publication available every Monday morning at various distribution points throughout London. Pick up a copy as soon as you can on Monday because they are snapped up quickly. The magazine is also available on subscription.
TNT Magazine: www.tntmag.co.uk
14–15 Child's Place
Earls Court
London SW5 9RX, UK
Tel: (020) 7373 3377
Fax: (020) 7341 6600

TNT Magazine produces two independent travellers' guides for Australians, New Zealanders and South Africans in the UK. They are: *Great Britain and Ireland Independent Travellers' Guide* and *London International Travellers' Guide*. The publishers of *TNT Magazine* also publish **Southern Cross**, targeted at the growing number of professional Australians, New Zealanders and South Africans who live in London. The publication is available free on Wednesdays.

New Zealand News UK and ***South Africa Times UK*** are expatriate newspapers published for the vast number of New Zealanders and South Africans on working holidays in the UK. They are free from various outlets in London every Wednesday. They include news from home and information about accommodation, recruitment, etc., in the UK. *New Zealand News UK* is available on subscription.
South Africa Times UK: www.satimesuk.co.uk
New Zealand News UK: www.nznewsuk.co.nz
Commonwealth Publishing Ltd
3rd Floor, New Zealand House
80 Haymarket
London SW1Y 4TE, UK
Tel: (020) 7747 9200

Travel clubs are good starting points for working holidaymakers. For a small joining fee they offer services like: mail holding; luggage storage; all your travel needs; e.g. booking airfares, tours and travel insurance; links to budget accommodation; advice on finding work; and

have noticeboards with relevant information. Some provide access to computers to type up your CV or surf the Internet. Here is a selection:
The Backpacker Co.: www.backpacker.co.uk
22 Conduit Place
London W2 1HS, UK
(nearest Tube station: Paddington)
Tel: (020) 7706 1539
Fax: (020) 7706 1538

Contiki
Contiki has a club, travel and information centre in the Royal National Hotel, London, for those going on its tours. Refer to a European tour brochure for more details.

Deckers London Club
Top Deck Travel
131–135 Earls Court Road
London SW5 9RH, UK
(nearest Tube station: Earls Court)
Tel: (020) 7370 4555
Fax: (020) 7370 6487

Drifters
22 Craven Terrace
London W2 3QH, UK
(nearest Tube station: Paddington)
Tel: (020) 7402 9171
Fax: (020) 7706 2673

Global Travel Team: www.globaltravelteam.com
16 Mortimer Street
London W1N 7RD, UK
(nearest Tube station: Oxford Circus)
Tel: (020) 7580 2939
Fax: (020) 7580 1239

London Walkabout Club: www.walkaboutclub.com
68–70 North End Road
London W14 0SJ, UK
(nearest Tube station: West Kensington)
Tel: (020) 7602 4392
Fax: (020) 7602 6433

Travellers Contact Point: www.travellers.com.au
2–6 Inverness Terrace
Bayswater
London W2 3HY, UK
(nearest Tube station: Bayswater)
Tel: (020) 7243 7887
Fax: (020) 7243 7888

For more detailed information on living, working and playing in the UK refer to *Live, Work and Play in London and the UK* published by Kangaroo Press.

UNITED STATES OF AMERICA

Unfortunately, the United States of America (USA) does not have any working holiday schemes, which limits opportunities for obtaining work to a pre-arranged program, transfer by your current employer or by applying to go in the Green Card Lottery.

There are three programs available: the Au Pair Program, which allows you a stay of up to one year to work as an au pair; the Summer Camp Program, in which most obtain a position as a camp counselor for three months over the summer vacation; and the Resort America program, which allows full-time students from the southern hemisphere to undertake work in ski resorts throughout America for four months (November to March). These programs have been authorised by the US government to help you obtain the J-1 visa, allowing you to enter the USA, under certain restrictions, to legally undertake the specific work of the program. For more information see the 'Programs' section in Chapter 5.

To work full-time in the USA you will need a Green Card, which gives the holder the legal right to live, work and study permanently in the USA. Every year, the Department of State allocates a certain number of Green Cards for issue to citizens from a number of eligible countries. You must enter the **Green Card Lottery** (officially known as the 'Diversity Visa Lottery') to obtain a Green Card.

If you apply and are selected, you will receive a Green Card and be allowed to live and work legally in the USA. It doesn't affect your present citizenship, but Green Card holders are allowed to apply for citizenship of the USA.

The registration period for the Diversity Visa Lottery (DV-2001) occurs in October of each year; there is no fee for applying. Refer to the US Department of State's Bureau of Consular Affairs Department website at http://travel.state.gov/dv2001.html for details.

National Visa Center
Portsmouth NH [insert relevant zip code—see below]
Tel: (0603) 334 0700 (automated recorded message system open 24 hours a day. Operators available from 9am to 4.45pm EST Monday through Thursday). If intending to contact the centre using the postal address above, the zip code to use is the one from the region of nativity; for example, if from Asia insert 00210, if from Europe insert 00212, Africa is 00213; Oceania is 00214 (this includes Australia, New Zealand, New Guinea and the islands of the South Pacific) and North America is 00215.

The Department of State's website advises that there is only one centre, the National Visa Centre, where you should apply to enter the Green Card Lottery. It also says that there are a number of organisations with similar names to the National Visa Centre who say they can give you an advantage over other applicants by allowing them to help you with your application. Of course, there is a fee for them doing this. These organisations are mostly immigration specialists and the National Visa Centre advises you not to use them.

When I searched the Internet for information on the Green Card Lottery, a number of these organisations came up. It is your choice as to whether you decide to use one, but there is no harm in contacting them for more information about the lottery. Here are the contact details for one of them:

National Visa Service: www.dv-2001.com
4200 Wisconsin Avenue, NW
Washington DC 20016, USA
Tel: (0202) 298 5600
Fax: (0202) 298 5601

It should be noted that US employers are legally required to check prospective employees papers to confirm they are either American citizens or aliens with the appropriate authorisation allowing them to work. However, there are some employers who will pay cash-in-hand because they claim they cannot find Americans to do the job. If your employer is caught employing an illegal alien, they will receive a hefty fine. If you are the illegal employee, you can expect to be deported and unable to travel to the US in the future. It is suggested that if you hope to find (illegal) work in the US that you speak with other travellers who are 'in the know'.

Most travellers looking for jobs usually head to the major cities of Los Angeles, San Francisco, New York, Chicago, Washington, etc., where there are many opportunities. These include office-based positions, hospitality positions in bars, cafes, hostels and hotels, labouring, etc. Most find positions by registering with specialist employment agencies, via hostel noticeboards or through major newspapers including *USA Today*, *The Boston Globe*, *Chicago Tribune*, *Los Angeles Times*, *New York Times*, *Village Voice* (New York), *San Francisco Chronicle* and *Washington Post*.

Holiday centres, such as along the Florida coast, will provide a number of hospitality positions. It is suggested that you pick up travel brochures on the specific area you wish to work. Here you will find a list of accommodation available. Each will mention the services they have to offer. Depending on the size of the establishment these can include cafes, restaurants, beauty parlours, fitness centres, swimming pools, tennis courts, etc. You could then apply for a specific position, or a number of positions, directly to the accommodation as you will have its full contact details in the brochure.

Popular ski centres such as Aspen in Colorado can also yield a number of hospitality positions. For more information refer to the 'Ski centres' section in Chapter 7.

Another popular place to find hospitality work would be in Las Vegas. This could be a croupiers' paradise.

Many people go to the USA to learn English, therefore, there are opportunities to teach English. Those who hold the University of Cambridge/Royal Society of Arts Courses (Cambridge/RSA) Certificate or the Trinity Certificate in Teaching English from Trinity College do have an advantage to landing the best jobs. Refer to 'Teaching English' in the 'Teaching' section in Chapter 7.

Nurses are able to work in the US after completing and passing an examination. Refer to the 'Allied health' section in Chapter 7.

CHAPTER 7

A–Z of jobs

ACCOUNTING, BANKING AND FINANCIAL SERVICES

This section covers a wide variety of positions in a number of fields. It is therefore hard to list exact details of what work you can find as you travel the world. It is suggested you contact the specialist employment agencies listed in this section who can advise you of the latest industry trends and available positions.

If you currently work in the accounting, banking and financial service fields in a major international company, you may wish to see if there is an opportunity for a transfer to another country.

There are two major countries in which working holidaymakers find positions in these fields. They are the UK (for Commonwealth citizens) and Australia (for British, Irish, New Zealanders and Canadians). For those with an EU passport there are many opportunities arising in the European Union member states.

Your qualifications are recognised in these countries and you do not need to register with an official body to practice. Positions can be found at all levels and in many specialities.

Temporary and contract positions are available through employment agencies who specialise in placing you in such positions. These firms advertise in major papers, in industry journals, in the free backpacker magazines and the free general office magazines which are handed out at train and Tube stations.
- In the UK: *TNT Magazine, Southern Cross, New Zealand News UK, Ms London, Girl About Town, Nine to Five* and *Midweek*.
- In Australia: *Aussie Backpacker, TNT Magazine Australia, Nine to Five* and *City Weekly*.

You will find positions on the **Careermosaic**, **Monsterboard** and **www.accountingjobs.com** websites.

The following agencies specialise in placing accountancy and finance professionals in a number of fields, including commerce and industry, banking and financial, chartered accountancy, management consultancy, and public services and charities. Positions are available on a temporary, contract or permanent basis.

Some agencies have offices in Australia and the UK to cater for the huge amount of working holidaymakers who move between these two countries, but many of them also have offices throughout the world. Their websites include a listing of current positions which can be applied for on-line. The agencies have liaison officers who can provide information and advice on working in other countries, particularly the UK and Australia.

Australasian Temp Company: www.australasian-temps.co.uk

Australia
Level 5, BHP House
1 Castlereagh St
Sydney NSW 2000
Tel: (02) 9221 0900
Fax (02) 9221 0500

United Kingdom
125–129 Cheapside
London EC2V 6ll
Tel: (020) 7500 1709
Fax: (020) 7500 2133

New Zealand

Auckland:
Tel: (09) 357 9800
Fax: (09) 357 9801

Christchurch:
Tel: (03) 374 9222
Fax: (03) 374 9223

Wellington:
Tel: (04) 472 4157
Fax: (04) 471 0958

FSS Financial: www.fssfinancial.co.uk

Australia
Level 65, MLC Centre
19–29 Martin Place
Sydney NSW 2000
Tel: (02) 9235 3222
Fax: (02) 9235 3999

New Zealand
10b Kamahi Place
Christchurch 5
Tel: (03) 359 5216
Fax: (03) 359 3356

South Africa
Johannesburg:
PO Box 847
Riverclub, Johannesburg
Tel/Fax: (011) 883 4413

Durban:
PO Box 1311
Kloof, Durban 3640
Tel/Fax: (031) 764 6065

United Kingdom
Charlotte House
14 Windmill Street
London W1P 2DY
Tel: (020) 7209 1000
Fax: (020) 7209 0001

HW Group: www.working-holidays.co.uk

Australia:
Level 9, 66 Hunter Street
Sydney NSW 2000
Tel: (02) 9510 1444
Fax: (02) 9510 1440
www.hwgroup.com/au

Republic of Ireland
10 Lower Mount Street
Dublin 2
Tel: (01) 676 5000
Fax: (01) 676 5111

United Kingdom
Cardinal House, 39–40 Albermarle Street
Green Park, London W1X 4ND
Tel: (020) 7629 4463
Fax: (020) 7491 4705

Michael Page: www.mpage.com.au

Australia and New Zealand
Level 19, 1 York Street
Sydney NSW 2000
Tel: (02) 9254 0200
Fax: (02) 9254 0333

Hong Kong and China
601, One Pacific Place, 88 Queensway
Hong Kong
Tel: (02) 2530 2000
Fax: (02) 2530 2250

Singapore
24 Raffles Place
17–05 Clifford Centre
Singapore
Tel: (65) 533 2777
Fax: (65) 533 7227

United Kingdom
Page House, 39–41 Parker Street
London WC2B 5LN
Tel: (020) 7831 2000
Fax: (020) 7430 2011

Robert Walters plc: www.robertwalters.com

Australia
Level 10, 3 Bridge Street
Sydney NSW 2000
Tel: (02) 9241 7455
Fax: (02) 9241 7466

New Zealand
Level 11, Microsoft House
Symonds Street
Auckland
Tel: (09) 302 2280
Fax: (09) 302 4930

South Africa
West Tower, 2nd Floor
Sandton Square, Maude Street
Sandown, Johannesburg
Tel: (011) 881 5417
Fax: (011) 881 5516

United Kingdom
10 Bedford Street
London WC2E 9HE
Tel: (020) 7379 3333
Fax: (020) 7915 8714

AGRICULTURE AND FARMING

You could write a whole book on the various agricultural areas of the world! Unfortunately (or fortunately for myself), we don't have the room in this guide, but I have tried to provide as much information as possible on programs and areas where work can be found.

Firstly though, I'd like to emphasise the importance of looking at what region you will be working in. By surveying your surroundings you can identify what agricultural/farming work may be available. For instance, are there orchards, vegetables, other crops or livestock around? Planting or picking fruit and vegetables may then be available (if it is the right season) or work driving tractors, mending fences, irrigating fields, tending to animals, etc., could be found.

Agricultural programs

If you have a background in farming and are interested in working abroad you may wish to contact the **International Agricultural Exchange Association (IAEA)**. IAEA can help find overseas jobs for those with genuine experience in agriculture and horticulture between the ages of 18 and 30.

There are a number of programs available including those in agriculture, horticulture, home management (household), agri-mix (agriculture and household) and hort-mix (horticulture and household). Programs can last from six to 18 months and are available in many European countries, as well as Japan, Canada, the USA, Australia and New Zealand.

IAEA has a very good website, which will answer all your questions. The site also lists the contact details of IAEA's offices:

IAEA: www.Agexchange.asn.au/~iaea/

Australia
Suite 203, Level 2
65 York Street
Sydney NSW 2000
Tel: (02) 9299 5300
Fax: (02) 9299 0847

Canada
#105, 7710–5 Street SE
Calgary, Alberta
Tel: (0403) 255 7799
Fax: (0403) 225 6024

Denmark
V. Farimagsgade 6
DK-1606 Kobenhavn V.
Tel: (033) 91 66 88
Fax: (033) 91 58 58

Japan
IAEA Servicing Officer
Doelaoyagi 2–203
Aoyagi 521, Maebashi, Gunma 371
Tel: (0272) 356 923
Fax: (0272) 355 583

New Zealand
Park Lane Arcade
The Strand, Box 328
Whakatane
Tel: (07) 307 0086
Fax: (07) 307 1137

United Kingdom
The Y.F.C. Centre
National Agricultural Centre
Kenilworth
Warwickshire CV8 2LG
Tel: (01203) 696 578
Fax: (01203) 696 684

USA
1000-1st Avenue South
Great Falls
Montana 59401
Tel: (0406) 727 1999
Fax: (0406) 727 1997

WWOOF (Willing Workers on Organic Farms)

If you would like to experience life working on an organic farm you could 'WWOOF' your way around the world. It should be noted that WWOOF is an exchange program and is not a source of paid employment. In exchange for your willingness to work you will receive food and lodging, and gain first-hand knowledge of your host's agricultural methods and way of life. It is not necessary to be experienced or qualified.

As being a WWOOFer is a cultural experience and one which you are not being paid to do, you do not need a work permit or working holiday visa to enjoy it. Therefore you could WWOOF in as many countries as you'd like.

As farms range from self-sufficient holdings through to full commercial operations, duties are wide and varied. You may find yourself making mud bricks, sowing crops, milking cows or goats, feeding chickens, chopping wood, planting, composting, and making cheese and yoghurt. You may also be able to find some other situations, such as child minding and typing.

WWOOF organisations exist in a number of countries. Each produces its own list of WWOOF-participating host farms. Before you can be accepted onto a host farm, you must become a member of the WWOOF organisation. Each organisation also has its own membership arrangements, so contact one of the representatives listed below (do include return postage or an International Reply Coupon to cover postage).

WWOOF: www.phdcc.com/sites/wwoof (this site is linked to individual-country WWOOF sites).

Australia
Lionel Pollard
Mt Murrindal Co-op
Buchan Vic 3885
Tel: (03) 5155 0218

Austria
Hildegard Gottleib
Langegg 155
851 St Stefan ob Stainz

Canada
John Vanden Heuvel
RR2 Carlson Rd
Nelson, BC, V1L 5P5
Tel: (0604) 354 4417

Denmark
Bent and Inga Nielsen
Assenjev 35
9881 Bindslev

Finland
Riita-Leena Makinen
Koikkalanmylly
51880 Koikkala
Tel: (055) 450 251

Germany
Miriam Wittmann
Postfach 210259
01263 Dresden

Ireland
Kieran and Rose O'Brien
Harpoonstown, Drinagh
Co. Wexford
Tel: (053) 35395

Italy
Bridgett Matthews
109 via Casavecchia
57022 Castagneto
Carducci, LI

Japan
Glenn and Kiyoko Burns
Akebono 5-Jo 3-Chome 19-17
Teine-ku, Sapporo, 006

Korea
Chang Yul
Lee KPO Box 1516
Seoul 110-601

New Zealand
Jane and Andrew Strange
PO Box 1172
Nelson
Tel/Fax: (03) 544 9890

Switzerland
Postfach 59
8124 Maur

United Kingdom
Fran Whittle
PO Box 2675
Lewes
Sussex BN17 1RB
Tel: (01273) 476 286

Australian farm work

Australia offers a number of farming options. There are the above-mentioned programs, along with jackarooing or jillarooing on outback properties.

JACKAROO/JILLAROO
If you want to experience real outback life, then you may want to try working as a jackaroo or jillaroo on an outback Australian cattle or sheep station.

Most of these outback stations are in Queensland, the Northern Territory and the Kimberley region of Western Australia where a farm size of well over a million hectares is not uncommon. Work in the northern states is mostly available from March to October; during the hot, wet summer months of November to March the stations only maintain a skeleton staff.

Duties will depend on the position you fill and also on what kind of farm/station it is. Stations usually run cattle, and pastoral companies farm wheat and sheep. So you could be rounding up stock, either on horseback (for cattle) or motorbike (sheep), feeding stock, drenching stock, mending fences, etc. Experience isn't always necessary but is useful.

Positions are often found through hostel noticeboards or through newspapers such as *The Land*. You could also try **Outback Staff**, based in Rockhampton, Queensland, on Tel: (07) 4927 4300, for positions in Queensland, the Northern Territory and the Kimberleys; and for positions nationwide, **Rural Enterprises**, Tel: (08) 9325 8411. Website address: www.ruralenterprises.com.au

There are a number of farms which provide a short training course, involving farm work, followed by placement on a farm.

The longest established course is the **Visitoz Scheme**, which invites students and travellers to gain a taste of farm or station life as a working jackaroo/jillaroo.

The scheme is run by Dan and Joanna Burnet on their 510-hectare cattle property, Springbrook Host Farm, which is about 280 km north-west of Brisbane—a bus from Brisbane passes the front gate five times a week in each direction and will stop on request.

Training at Springbrook, or one of the associate farms, covers tractor driving, ag-bike, horse riding, cattle handling and useful skills such as fencing and scrub clearing. Once you have completed the course, the Burnets will offer you a choice of the suitable jobs available.

Don't forget your sunhat, sunscreen and long-sleeved shirts, boots, jeans, alarm clock and pen knife.

Visitoz Scheme

Australia
Dan and Joanna Burnet
Springbrook
via Goomeri Qld 4601
Tel: (07) 4168 6106
Fax: (07) 4168 6155

London
William or Gemma Taunton-Burnet
Tel/Fax: (020) 8748 0046
Mobile: 0966 528 644

Scotland
Anne Beckitt
Tel: (01866) 844 271

Scandinavia and Baltic countries
Lars Hakan Eriksson
universea@mbox200.swipnet.se

Japan
Kasue Ozawa, Tokyo
Tel: (03) 3352 8837
Fax: (03) 3352 3635

UK farm work
Farm positions are advertised in the *New Zealand News UK* and *Farmers Weekly*. Also contact the following agencies:

Bligh Appointments
70 North End Road
London W14 9EP
Tel: (020) 7603 6123
Fax: (020) 7371 6898

Fletchers Relief Services: Tel: (01296) 655 777

Farmforce: Tel: (01432) 279 933
The UK also offers some unusual seasonal opportunities. At Christmastime people are required to help pluck turkeys. The summer season sees the 'rich and famous' come out to play, creating opportunities to bait salmon hooks for fishermen, or to become a 'beater', where you go into the woods to flush out pheasants and deer for shooters to practise their shots. There are also opportunities to be a shepherd during the spring lambing season.

Fruit and vegetable picking

Fruit and vegetable picking is not just about picking fruit and vegetables to send to markets, factories, wineries and canneries. Though picking time is usually the period during which most travellers find work, there are other things outside the harvest time to be done—planting, fertilising, pruning, etc. So if you miss the picking work there may be other jobs available.

If you have never picked fruit and vegetables before, the first few days will be a learning experience. This is very strenuous work. I have met travellers who refuse to 'do that type of work again', but I have also met those who have loved it and continue to do it.

Each position can differ greatly. You may be picking root vegetables (where you are continually bending over) or climbing up ladders or in a mechanical hoist to reach fruit in trees.

Be prepared to rise early and to work in all types of weather, although work usually stops during wet weather (though this can depend on the grower).

Before you agree to take a position, you should confirm the number of hours you are required to work (including the starting time), the rate of pay (whether by piece work or on an hourly rate), when you will be paid and how often, what kind of accommodation is available (if any is provided), whether meals are provided or if you have to cook your own (some farms are isolated and so provide accommodation and meals), and whether you are required to bring your own tools, such as secateurs and buckets.

As with all outdoor work, you will sometimes have to put up with bad weather or blistering sun. Check with the farmer and other pickers about appropriate clothing. Wear a hat and sunscreen in sunny weather. Fingerless gloves and thermal underwear are useful in cold weather as too many layers of clothes can be cumbersome.

Following is a list of some harvests around the world, country by country. Harvest dates are approximate only and vary due to seasonal factors (which can make it hard if you have turned up in a remote area and have either missed the start or have to wait a few weeks for the harvest to begin).

As vast numbers of people are required to complete harvests, farmers may overlook the fact that some travellers do not have the appropriate paperwork. Be warned that authorities are well aware of the popularity of this work among illegal workers and can make raids to catch those without the proper documentation.

AUSTRALIA
Australia provides an abundance of year-round fruit and vegetable picking. So if you want to follow the sun and top up your travel funds, then there are plenty of opportunities for doing so.

Now I could easily list the fruit and vegetable picking areas here. Unfortunately, there are literally hundreds of them so it's best to find out about the harvests yourself. Here's how. First, there have been a couple of books written on fruit and vegetable picking in Australia. They not only have information on individual harvests but suggest accommodation, places to eat and visit and include many contact details. These are available in good bookstores in Australia. Harvest guides are also published in the free backpacker magazines, *Aussie Backpacker* and *TNT Magazine Australia*. The government employment service, Employment National, also produces a harvest guide. You can contact the Employment National harvest hotline (1300 720 126) or contact the nearest Employment National office in the area you wish to work and find out approximate harvest starting dates.

There are working hostels. These hostels have associations with local growers, so when you stay at a working hostel the farmer, or the hostel, provides a lift to and from the orchards each day. Bundaberg (home of Bundaberg Rum) in northern Queensland provides year-round banana and sugar-cane work (both are very strenuous), and has many working hostels. Most working hostels advertise regularly in backpacker magazines. You could also contact:

Harvest Helpers: Tel: (02) 6452 2172 (for work in New South Wales)

Outsource Personnel: www.outsourcepersonnel.com.au
For work in Queensland: Brisbane Tel: (07) 3252 2883
Toowoomba Tel: (07) 4638 4699
For work in New South Wales: Dubbo Tel: (02) 6811 6330
Griffith Tel: (02) 6962 9888

CANADA

The Okanagan Valley in British Colombia stretches over some 200 km and supports around 12,000 hectares of orchards, where peaches, pears, plums, cherries, apricots, apples and grapes are grown. The major areas within the valley where travellers find picking work are Armstrong, Vernon, Kelowna, Peachland, Summerland, Penticton, Okanagan Falls, Oliver, Sooyoos and Keremeos.

Most of the harvesting work is done over the northern hemisphere summer months. Beginning dates vary from area to area but start around June and can end as late as November.

In Ontario you could try around the Niagara area, Chatham and Leamington especially, where peaches, pears, plums, cherries and tomatoes are grown. Some travellers find work planting trees during the tree-planting season which runs from April to July.

The **Agricultural Employment Service (AES)** has offices in major centres of these areas and offers good advice on fruit picking.

EUROPE

It is very hard to find legal work without proper EU recognition. Farmers, however, can turn a blind eye to this because they need their crops picked.

The new international EURES employment service may be able to help you.

France is a huge attraction for many travellers and is usually the first stop after leaving the UK. France offers an abundance of picking work, particularly in the grape harvest areas of Bordeaux, Champagne, Beaujolais and Burgundy during September and October.

Although a lot of travellers find positions in these major areas, some find it easier to look for work in smaller areas where there is less competition with other travellers. France's national employment agency, Agence Nationale pour L'Emploi (ANPE) (www.anpe.fr/accuel.htm), has offices in major harvest areas which may help you. Also look on noticeboards in hostels.

Greece is regarded by travellers as a 'party paradise', but for those who spend all their money, picking work can be found. As I've mentioned before, have a look at the environment of the area you are in. Particular islands where picking work can be found include Crete, Rhodes and Cyprus.

The best way to find work is to ask around in the area or look on hostel noticeboards.

UNITED KINGDOM

The UK offers the traveller a number of opportunities to pick fruit and vegetables. The principal picking areas are in Kent, East Anglia, and the South and West country.

There is year-round picking work available but personally, I don't know if I'd want to be doing it during the cold weather!

The free weekly *TNT Magazine* and *New Zealand News UK* are two good sources where fruit and vegetable picking positions are advertised. Some agencies to contact include:

Bligh Appointments Tel: (020) 7603 6123

Staffing Solutions Tel: (01760) 720 888 (for fruit and vegetable picking in the Norfolk area)

ALLIED HEALTH (INCLUDING NURSING)

'Allied health' is the name given to cover all health professionals who work in hospitals. This section covers work opportunities in a number of countries for nurses, doctors, physiotherapists, speech therapists, radiographers, podiatrists, etc.

To practise in your medical field in another country often means needing your qualifications recognised by the governing body in that country. The processes involved in having your qualifications recognised can be time-consuming and costly. Sometimes you may be required to undertake extra training before your qualifications can be recognised. Fortunately, there are many agencies who can help you gain registration and offer employment on a temporary or contract basis.

There are, however, other work possibilities available which you may like to consider. For instance, there are positions for medical staff on cruise liners or on summer camps, or you could volunteer to do aid work. You may consider being a nanny or a carer where some of your skills could be put to good use. Refer to the appropriate sections for more information on these positions.

The main countries where allied health staff find work are in Australia, the United Kingdom, the Middle East and in the United States. Many specialist agencies who can help you find a position in another country often advertise in union magazines and newspapers. Some also advertise in major newspapers.

Australia

Australia's working holiday visa is available for one year, which does limit professional allied health workers finding positions as registration can be time-consuming and costly.

Many nurses obtain their registration. Each Australian State requires nurses to be registered with that State to practise. Most nurses obtain their registration in New South Wales then find a position through one of the many specialist nursing agencies which can find positions in major hospitals in Sydney and in country New South Wales areas. It is worth noting that registration can be rolled over to other States, allowing nurses to work there. Registration can be obtained in two ways, by either attending the Board's office in person or submitting your documents by mail to:

Nurses Registration Board

Postal address
PO Box K599
Haymarket NSW 1238

Street address
Level 2, 28 Foveaux Street
Surry Hills NSW 2010
Tel: (02) 9219 0222

A huge number of specialist nursing employment agencies advertise in the Australian independent travellers' magazines: *Aussie Backpacker* and *TNT Magazine Australia*. Refer to their details under the Australian area analysis in Chapter 6.

Middle East

Western nurses are highly prized in the Middle East. You will be required to undertake a minimum one-year contract.

Meditemp International recruits general and specialised nursing personnel, medical consultants and allied health professionals for positions in the Middle East.

Meditemp International: www.choice.net.au

Choice Personnel
PO Box 7108
Cloisters Square
Perth WA 6850
Tel: (08) 9321 2066
Fax: (08) 9321 1113

Canada toll-free: 0800 993 062
NZ toll-free: 0800 442 314
UK toll-free: 0800 893 496

MH Matrix International Recruitment recruits general and specialist doctors, nurses, medical scientists, physiotherapists, radiographers, dentists and medical secretaries for positions in Middle Eastern hospitals.

MH Matrix International Recruitment: www.mhmatrix.com

Australia
Level 9, Charles Plaza
66 King Street
Sydney NSW 2000
Tel: (02) 9262 4739
Fax: (02) 9262 5599

New Zealand
36 Omahu Road
Remerah
Auckland
Tel: (09) 524 6035
Fax: (09) 9524 6095

United Kingdom

The United Kingdom has a shortage of nurses and other allied health professionals. UK hospitals love Australian, New Zealand, Canadian and South African nurses.

For those who do not qualify for the appropriate working holiday visa, it is possible to qualify for a work permit when you agree to a contract position of six months to one year. You must obtain registration before you can practise in National Health Service (NHS) hospitals.

Chiropodists, dietitians, medical laboratory scientists, occupational therapists, orthoptists, physiotherapists and radiographers must register with **The Council for Professions Supplementary to Medicine**:

The Registrar [*of your profession/s*] Board
Park House, 184 Kennington Park Road
London SE11 4BU
Tel: (020) 7582 0866
Fax: (020) 7820 9684

Social workers' qualifications must be validated by:
Council for Education and Training in Social Work (CETSW)
Derbyshire House, St Chad's Street
London WC1 H8AD
Tel: (020) 7278 2454

Nurses must register with the **UKCC (United Kingdom Central Council for Nursing, Midwifery and Health Visiting)** at:
Registrations Manager
23 Portland Place
London W1N 4JT
Tel: (020) 7637 7181
Fax: (020) 7436 2924

A huge number of specialist nursing employment agencies advertise in the UK *TNT Magazine*. Refer to their details under the UK area analysis in Chapter 6.

As the UK is a big drawcard for Australian, New Zealand and South African nurses, there are a number of specialist nursing and allied health agencies with offices or contacts in these countries. Get in touch with them to obtain information and help on working as a nurse in the UK. Some of these agencies can also find placements for you before you leave your home country.

BMG Associates has been helping allied health professionals from the Commonwealth find temporary and contract positions in the UK since 1990.

BMG Associates: www.bmgassociates.com.au

Australia	*New Zealand*
PO Box 2304	61 Malvern Road
Fitzroy MDC Vic 3065	Mt Albert
Tel: (03) 9416 2333	Auckland 1003
Fax: (03) 9416 2399	Tel: (09) 849 3854
Toll-free: 1800 677 948	Fax: (09) 849 3854
	Toll-free: 0800 803 854

Nightingale Nursing Bureau has offices in Australia and the UK and can help nurses with positions in either country.
Nightingale Nursing Bureau

Australia	*United Kingdom*
Milsons Village, Suite 13	2 Tavistock Place
48 Alfred Street	London WC1H 9RA
Milsons Point NSW 2061	Tel: (020) 7833 3952
Tel: (02) 9964 9266	Fax: (020) 7278 4067
Fax: (02) 9964 9449	

NMS recruits nursing staff for the UK and the USA.
NMS

Australia
Suite 103, Walker House
161 Walker Street
North Sydney NSW 2060
Tel: (02) 9956 7533
Fax: (02) 9956 7833
Toll-free: 1800 357533

New Zealand
Toll-free: 0800 445582

USA

To nurse in the USA you must sit an exam. Firstly, you will need to submit your documents to the Board of Nursing in the US state you wish to nurse. Processing can take three months. Once you meet all the requirements, you will be issued with an Authorisation to Test (ATT) by the NCLEX (National Council Licensing Exam). The ATT is valid for three months. You must sit the exam on US soil.

If you do not have US citizenship, you will need to be sponsored for a work visa. Contact a specialist employment agency who can help you with gaining your registration and a sponsored position. Refer to NMS's details above.

CARE WORK

You do not necessarily need to be qualified, experienced or female to do care work. As long as you are caring, patient, honest and reliable there could be a position helping an elderly person or persons stay in their home, helping someone while they convalesce or aiding a disabled person.

You may be called upon to shower and dress your charge, help them on the toilet, cook their meals, do the housework, drive them to the hairdresser's or golf or wherever they wish to go, or just be around for company.

Assignments can vary in length; you may even be on rotating shifts with other carers. Positions can be live-in, where you may only have one client to look after, or live-out, where you may visit a number of clients each day.

In Australia contact:
Dial-an-Angel: Tel: (02) 9416 7511

There are a number of specialist care agencies in the United Kingdom. They advertise in *TNT Magazine* and *The Lady*.

CARGO/FREIGHTER SHIP POSITIONS

Many travellers have been able to work their passage on cargo/freighter ships. If you are interested in doing this, there are many companies with ships sailing the world on set routes.

I have seen a number of books published on the subject which you may wish to borrow from a library. Also look at shipping schedules in newpapers.

Some travellers find a position by speaking to the captain or other crew members, or by contacting the office in the port.

Many cargo/freight ship companies are now offering passenger services. One website I found mentions such companies, the nationality of the owners, their sailing schedules, and which ports they sail from and to. This site is really aimed at people who wish to travel as passengers on cargo/freight lines, but the contact details could be used to determine whether or not you would like to work for them. Website address: www.freighter-cruises.com

CRUISE-LINE POSITIONS

As recently as 30 years ago, people endured long sea voyages as a means to reach other countries. Nowadays people go on a cruise for sheer pleasure and indulgence. Today's ocean liners—often referred to as 'floating hotels'—require vast numbers of staff for efficient operation. Some large and luxurious cruise liners need around 2,000 crew to run smoothly. Staff are required in the following areas:

- officers: captain, ship's mates, cruise director;
- office support: clerk, cashier, receptionist;
- maintenance: engineers, electricians, painters, plumbers;
- hospitality: bellboy, dishwasher, cabin steward, chefs, bar attendants, waiting staff;
- entertainers: singer, dancer, juggler, comedian, film projectionist, musicians, DJ;
- child carers: nanny, babysitter;
- medical staff: doctor, nurse, dentist;
- other: shop assistants, croupiers, laundry staff, photographers, security officers;
- health and beauty: hairdresser, beautician, aerobic instructor, gym instructor, masseuse.

In general, you do not need to have worked on a cruise liner previously to obtain work, but this does depend on individual cruise lines. Having experience in a field is more highly regarded than having qualifications in that field. Even without experience positions can still be obtained.

The minimum age is usually 18 or 21, with no upper age limit. For those travellers who do not qualify for a working holiday scheme or program this may be an option. Cruise lines prefer to have experienced staff, and the older you are, it is presumed the more experienced you will be in your field.

Main cruising areas

The main cruising areas are the Caribbean, Mediterranean and Aegean seas; the West Coast of America and Mexico; Alaska; the Norwegian fjords; the Pacific islands; and Asia. There are also liners that cross the Atlantic and those that sail around the world.

How to apply for a position

Cruise lines do not employ staff themselves. They rely on agencies and concessionaires to supply staff.

In researching this section I found that virtually each profession on a cruise liner is found through a different agency or concessionaire.

For instance, when I rang P&O in Sydney (who incidentally have a recorded message for those interested in working on P&O cruisers through the Pacific), I discovered that they use one concessionaire and/or agency to employ entertainers, one for security staff, another for medical staff, one for casino staff, one for hairdressers and another for photographers. Therefore, if you are looking for a position, it is essential to register with the appropriate concessionaire or agency. If you write directly to the cruise line it is likely that nothing will come of your application.

Now, not every cruise line uses the same concessionaire or agency for its staffing needs and, as you can imagine, there are quite a large number of them servicing different cruise lines. That's probably not what you wanted to read because finding a position is going to need some research on your part! So how do you find the correct concessionaire or agency to apply to? I suggest the following:

First, decide on the particular cruising area you are interested in, for example the Caribbean or the Pacific.

Secondly, find out what cruise liners sail in this area. Visit a travel agent and obtain cruise-line brochures.

Thirdly, find out what cruise-line company the liner belongs to. And fourthly, find out where the liner's home port is, and whether an office of this cruise-line company is in the home port.

Once you have established these things, contact the cruise-line company direct to find out what agency or concessionaire manages the particular type of employment you are looking for.

It is suggested that you apply for a specific position, for example bartender or pastry chef, rather than sending an application stating you want to apply for anything that is available. This is because when cruise lines require staff, say a bartender, they will contact the appropriate agency or concessionaire and request a person for that particular job and not someone who wants to do anything. Therefore, adapt your CV accordingly.

Life on board

On securing a position you will be required to sign a contract which can last for the length of the cruise or the cruise season. Most are for six months to one year. The contract should clearly state your position, length of contract, salary, hours, etc.

Forget about romantic notions of walking hand-in-hand along the deck at sunset. Working hours on cruise ships are often long and hard. You may be required to work seven days a week on fractured shifts, but this depends on your position and the cruise line.

New recruits can take a few days to gain their 'sea legs'. You will need to be aware of not only the passengers' safety but your own, and undertake lifeboat drills.

Accommodation is usually shared with other crew members. Crew cabins are often in the bowels of the ship or near the engine room!

Food on board should be excellent, and alcoholic drinks are charged at nominal prices. There may be recreational facilities provided solely for the crew, but this depends on the cruise line.

Finding work

To find out more information, you might consider buying a travel book that deals specifically with finding work on a cruise liner. These books are often self-published, so look in newspapers for advertisements and in bookshops.

You may also wish to purchase cruise-line magazines, in which cruise-line employment opportunities are often placed. Advertisements are also often placed in trade magazines, for example those aimed at hairdressers.

Most cruise lines have their own website. On investigation, I found these websites promote the luxuriousness of individual cruisers and the cruises available, including booking options. These websites do not mention work opportunities. You may wish to contact a specialist cruise-line employment agency.

Cruise Line Appointments was founded in 1991. They can help place candidates in a number of categories including:

- waiting staff (cocktail waiters, head waiters, busboys, etc.);
- chefs (pastry, sous, cooks, etc.);
- sales (fashion, jewellery, cosmetics, perfume, luxury goods, etc.);
- bar staff; purser; receptionists; shore-excursion; casino staff.

Cruise Line Appointments prefers you to have a minimum of two to three years' experience in your chosen field. You also need to be of excellent health, be well groomed and have a high standard of both written and spoken English.

You can send your CV and copies of your references to them or register on-line via their website. The registration fee is US$10.

Cruise Line Appointments: www.cruiselineappointments.com
142 Parkwood Road
Bournemouth
Dorset BH5 2BW, UK
Fax: (01202) 418787

CTI Group places candidates on cruise lines, cargo ships, in resorts, casinos and private clubs around the world.

You can contact CTI indicating the position or positions you are interested in. Include your CV and copies of professional certificates and qualifications. You can also register by going to the 'on-line application' section of their website.

CTI Group: www.cti-usa.com
Attention Human Resources Dept. WP2
1535 SE 17th Street — Suite 206
Fort Lauderdale, FL 33316, USA

EQUINE STAFF

If you have genuine experience in the equine industry (stable hand, track rider, show jumping, polo, dressage, eventing, etc.) and wish to use and improve your skills in Australia, New Zealand, the UK, Europe or the USA, a company called **Stablemate Staff Management** (and their associates) can place you in stable-/ranch-hand positions through their exchange program. The program includes organising the appropriate visa, your flight and a position. Positions are usually for 12 months, though some for six months are available. Contact the office in your home country.

If you are already in one of the countries mentioned and have the appropriate work visa, then contact the agencies below for permanent, temporary and casual equine positions.

There are also some positions in stable management and administration available.

Australia
Stablemate Staff Management: Tel: (02) 9654 9733 (Sydney)
Ireland
Equi People: Tel: (0502) 43195 (Co. Laois)
New Zealand
Rural Exchange NZ (RENZ): Tel: (03) 312 5181 (Christchurch)
South Africa
Worldwide Agri Exchange: Tel: (051) 436 6865 (Brandhorf)
United Kingdom
Stablemate Staff UK Ltd: Tel: (01572) 717 383 (Leicestershire)
USA
Communicating for Agriculture: Tel: (toll-free) 1800 432 3276 (Fergus Falls, MN)

FREELANCE JOURNALISM AND PHOTOGRAPHY

Many magazines and newspapers rely on freelance contributions to fill their pages. Travel editors in particular are always looking for well-written articles accompanied by good photographs. If you've read these pages and think you could write something too, then you most probably can, because you don't necessarily need to be a qualified journalist or photographer to supply articles or photos.

Before you send off articles, study the magazines and newspapers you want to approach. I suggest you contact the publication for their contributor guidelines. You may also wish to buy the publication and study the articles for the preferred style. There are books available listing possible markets and giving advice on how to get started. Look in the reference section in bookshops or try the library. The magazines listed in Chapter 5 take freelance articles. Contact them for their submission guidelines. You may also wish to contact the backpacker magazines (*Aussie Backpacker*, *New Zealand News UK*, *SA Times* and *TNT Magazine*) because they employ travellers in a variety of positions, including writers and journalists.

I don't know if you will get rich from supplying freelance articles and photographs, but it is a buzz to see your name in print—you might end up with memoirs, a coffee-table book or a travel guide!

HOLIDAY CAMPS
Europe and the United Kingdom

PGL Young Adventure provides children's adventure-based holidays. Established just over 40 years ago, it is named after its founder, Peter Gordon Lawrence. Each year, PGL recruits over 2,000 staff to

work in its centres in the UK, France and Spain. During winter there are ski programs in Europe. PGL requires staff as:
- group leaders, who take charge of groups of children outside activity times.
- activity instructors, who lead children in outdoor activities such as sailing or abseiling. You are required to hold a certificate to lead these activities. PGL provides the opportunity to obtain a nationally recognised qualification.

There are also positions for catering staff, support staff (domestic, maintenance, security, etc.), administrators, couriers (who lead coach trips to France and Spain), nurses and coach drivers.

PGL Young Adventure: www.pgl.co.uk
Seasonal Employment Department
Alton Court, Penyard Lane
Ross-on-Wye
Herefordshire HR9 5NR, UK
Tel: (01989) 767 833
Fax: (01989) 768 769

Travellers can also apply for PGL Young Adventure positions through STA Travel. Contact your nearest STA Travel office for details.

Village Camps was founded in 1972 and runs a number of educational and recreational programs for young people. There are camps in Austria (Zell), England (Hurstpierpoint in Sussex), France (Ardeche) and Switzerland (Leysin). All camps are in picturesque settings and offer a number of activities, including snow skiing and abseiling. Qualified instructors are required to lead these activities.

Village Camps: www.villagecamps.com
14, Rue de la Morache
CH-1260 NYON, Switzerland
Tel: (022) 990 9405
Fax: (022) 990 9494

Republic of Ireland

Delphi Adventure Holidays began in 1982. It is located in southwest Mayo, which is about 30 minutes from Galway on the west coast of the Republic of Ireland.

Delphi Adventure Holidays offers year-round adventure and education courses for students from primary and secondary schools, colleges and youth groups. It also has summer camp (July/August) for eight- to 17-year-olds. Other activities include corporate 'team building'.

Delphi Adventure Holidays requires qualified instructors to lead such activities as sailing, kayaking, windsurfing, canoeing, abseiling, rock climbing, archery, badminton, tennis and waterskiing. Catering staff are also required.

You will receive a weekly salary, food and accommodation. Staff are required during the season which runs between mid-February to mid-December. A minimum stay of two months is required.

Delphi Adventure Centre: www.delphiadventureholidays.ie
Leenane
Co. Galway, Ireland
Tel: (095) 42336
Fax: (095) 52303

USA

Of all the holiday camps around the world, the US summer camps are the best known. Every year, millions of American children between the ages of six and 16 attend summer camps (there have been many US movies made showing life on these camps which you may have seen).

There are around 12,000 of these camps, mostly in the north-east and upper mid-west of the USA, and they require young people aged 18 and over to undertake a variety of positions. If you like kids and want to spend around 16 weeks during the US summer (June to September) with them, then this may be for you.

Most join a camp as a 'counsellor' (spelt 'counselor' in the USA), either as a general counsellor (where you will supervise kids) or as a specialist counsellor (where you will supervise specific activities, such as swimming, crafts, horse riding, tennis and sailing).

Your days will be spent outdoors supervising kids, and nights around camp fires. Do note that you will be sharing your cabin with about a dozen of your charges.

If you would like to work at a camp but not be directly involved with the children, there are positions in administration, catering, maintenance and medicine. You can organise a place on a summer camp through a Summer Camp Program. The program includes: your placement in a camp; assistance with obtaining your J-1 visa; transport to the camp; accommodation and food for the length of your stay; pocket money; and time to travel after the camp is over.

These programs are very popular and the search for staff begins around September and closes in April for placements for the upcoming June. Lodge your application between September and April so you do not miss out.

There are a number of companies who have been authorised by the US government to place people from overseas in US summer camps.

Camp America: www.campamerica.co.uk

Australia
288a Whitehorse Road
Balwyn Vic 3103
Tel: (03) 9836 0111
Fax: (03) 9836 0149

New Zealand
PO Box 35-151
Naenae
Lower Hutt
Toll-free: 0800 872 967

United Kingdom
37A Queen's Gate
London SW7 5HR
Tel: (020) 7581 7373
Fax: (020) 7581 7377

Information and application forms can also be picked up at STA Travel offices.

Camp Counselors USA (CCUSA): www.campcounselors.com

Australia	Tel: (02) 9223 3366
Ireland	Tel: (01) 679 3735
New Zealand	Tel: (09) 575 7813
South Africa	Tel: (011) 783 0544
United Kingdom	Tel: (020) 8332 2952

International Exchange Programs (IEP) accepts applications for summer camps between September and May each year. Refer to its details in the 'Programs' section in Chapter 5.

HOSPITALITY

Hospitality is a growing industry and covers a whole gamut of positions. These include kitchen hands, chefs of all levels and specialties, waiting, bartending, front reception staff for hotels, housekeeping and porters.

These positions can be found in a wide variety of establishments, including cafes, cafeterias, fast-food outlets, diners, restaurants (licensed and unlicensed), nightclubs, function and convention centres, casinos, ski and seaside resorts, amusement parks, registered clubs, motels, hotels, guesthouses, caravan parks, airlines, railways and cruise liners.

Hospitality work can be found either by door-knocking or through specialist agencies which often advertise in the employment sections of major newspapers or backpacker magazines (including *TNT Magazine* and *Aussie Backpacker*). Some agencies have websites where the positions they have on offer are updated regularly.

Those without the appropriate visa often door-knock looking for cash work. These positions (such as dish washing) don't require qualifications or much experience on the applicant's behalf. If you have a specialist qualification (and the appropriate visa), for example as a chef, then you may wish to contact an employment agency.

It may be worth your while to take appropriate work clothes (black skirt or pants, a white shirt and a pair of flat, enclosed shoes). Depending on the establishment, you may be issued with a uniform, which could include a T-shirt emblazoned with the establishment's name and logo or corporate dress or theme dress (for example, traditional German dress).

Hospitality Online is an on-line career resource site specifically for those in the hospitality industry. I found current jobs listed with positions in the USA, Canada, Europe, Egypt, the Middle East, Asia and the Pacific. There was also an employer's directory. You can search for openings by position, by company and by location and apply for positions on-line. Website address: www.hospitalityonline.com

Amusement and theme parks

There are a number of amusement and theme parks around the world, including Disneyland, Sea World, Chessington World of Adventure (in the UK) and Movieworld (Gold Coast, Australia).

These parks offer a wide variety of positions. Staff are particularly required on weekends, during school holidays and during the summer months when more people 'come out to play'.

Staff are required to sell entrance tickets, to prepare and sell food in fast-food outlets and in restaurants, to sell merchandise, as ride attendants (mechanics are required to maintain rides), as cleaners, as entertainers, and to dress up in theme-character outfits. If live animals are at the park, animal handlers are required.

To find work you will need to contact the human resources section at the individual parks.

Bartending

Many people pick up bar work during their travels. The types of establishment where work can be found include a smoky local pub; a theme pub (American, Irish, Australian, etc.); self-brewing pubs; a nightclub; a restaurant; an exclusive hotel or casino; an ocean liner;

or a place in a particular area, such as a ski field or holiday resort. There are many possibilities if you have bar-work skills.

If you have never worked in a bar before, then consider gaining some experience in your local bar, even if you offer your services for free just to get some experience and obtain a reference. Or you could do a bar course and learn the 'recipes' for mixed drinks and cocktails. There are many establishments, however, who will take you on without any experience.

Bar work is best found by knocking on doors, by word of mouth from other travellers, through advertisements in the 'Hospitality' section of newspapers or backpacker magazines, and through specialist employment agencies.

Many travellers like to work in popular tourist areas, such as ski or beach resorts, for the added 'lifestyle perks', which could include a ski pass or the chance to lie around on the beach all day then work at night.

LIVE-IN BAR WORK IN THE UK

If you've heard the rumour that in the UK 'there's a pub on every corner'—well, it's true. Even if you haven't 'pulled a beer' before, guv'nors (the owners or managers of pubs) will often take you on (maybe on a trial basis) to see how you cope with serving crowds, using the tills and how well you interact with customers. There are also positions for couples.

Live-in bar work is popular. The hours can be long and often hard, but it is a great way to meet people. You will receive a small wage, accommodation (which might be your own or a shared room), and meals (usually only while you are on duty).

Many travellers prefer to stay in London where there is an abundance of bar positions, but jobs can be found all over the UK. If you want to leave London, you could work at a holiday destination on the Cornish coast, in the Lake District or in the Scottish Highlands.

Positions are advertised in the free weekly travellers' magazines *TNT Magazine*, *Southern Cross*, *SA Times* and *New Zealand News UK*. Many people just door-knock.

The **Original London Pub Company**, in association with STA Travel, offers young Australians and New Zealanders the opportunity to secure a job in a London pub before they leave home. Included in the scheme is a pre-arranged position; accommodation; a wage; and at least one meal a day. Contact STA Travel or the Original London Pub Company, Tel: (03) 9646 7673 (Melbourne number) or look at their website: www.londonpub.com.au

Chefs and cooks

If you are a part-qualified or fully qualified chef or cook you will be in demand in establishments around the world.

As you will be aware, there are many levels and specialities in the 'chef world', and positions can be found in cafes, in roadhouses, in major tourist centres, as a personal chef to a family, in casinos, on cruise liners and in a variety of eating establishments specialising in short orders, Italian, French, Tandoori, breakfast, etc.

Work can be found either by door-knocking, particularly for cafes, or through specialist employment agencies, of which there are many. These agencies advertise in the backpacker magazines and in the 'Catering' section of the employment pages in major newspapers. There are also many employment agencies with their own websites which list current positions and allow you to register on-line for these positions.

It may be worthwhile to take your own uniform (if questioned by customs officials, the uniform could be the fancy dress outfit you need for the tour you are taking!). You can purchase a uniform and a set of knives (if required) on the road.

Croupiers

If you are a qualified croupier, there are a few options available to you. Most find positions on the gaming tables in casinos. Casinos usually do their own recruiting, so you will need to apply directly to the casino in which you wish to work. Note that you will have to undertake a 'table test'. There are also opportunities on cruise liners, so refer to the 'Cruise-line positions' section earlier in this chapter.

Domestic staff

Domestic staff can include a housekeeper, butler or chauffeur working in a private home or in a five-star resort.

Note that positions in private homes are usually live-in. Most find a position by looking in newspaper classifieds, in magazines such as *The Lady* and *TNT Magazine* or by registering with an agency.

Festivals and sporting events

Festivals come in many shapes and forms. Some can be large and world-renowned (Olympics, Commonwealth Games, Edinburgh Comedy Festival, etc.), while others are local events.

Festivals provide plenty of job opportunities for travellers. These include setting up tents, marquees, tables and chairs; serving food;

manning stalls; and cleaning up afterwards (taking down tents and marquees, stacking chairs, pick up rubbish).

Sporting events can also yield work opportunities. Weekly events require staff to sell entrance tickets, fast food, merchandise, etc. Special events (such as F1 Grands Prix and tennis tournaments) also require such staff. You may be able to secure work by being 'on the spot' or through specialist employment agencies. Such events may yield work in associated services, for example accommodation.

Hostels

Most independent travellers stay at a hostel at some time during their travels. These hostels can provide more than just a cheap bed for the night. They are a great source of work.

You will find many hostels are staffed by travellers. Just by asking if there are positions available you could find yourself on reception welcoming new travellers to the establishment, cleaning the rooms, in the kitchen (if the hostel has one) or driving the courtesy minibus to pick up or drop off travellers from the airports, coach or train stations. This work is usually found by being in the right place at the right time. Become friendly with the staff already there and make it known that you are looking for work.

Hostels usually have a noticeboard which is a good source of job prospects. Local employers often contact hostels when they need staff as they know there will be travellers there eager for a day's work, no matter what it is.

Some examples of advertisements I have seen on hostel noticeboards are: umpire; swimming pool attendant; lawn mower; security guard; bartender at the races; tent and marquee erecter; circus-stall staffer; food preparer on a crocodile farm; telemarketer; telegram singer; leaflet dropper; handyman; courier; Santa Claus; house removalist; jackaroo/jillaroo; and fruit picker.

You may come across 'working hostels'. These are hostels which are associated with local employers who help you find work when you stay at the hostel. Working hostels are often found in fruit and vegetable picking areas. They often advertise in backpacker magazines.

Hotels and holiday resorts

There are vast numbers of staff required for the smooth operation of hotels and holiday resorts. These include front office staff, cashiers, receptionists, reservation clerks, car-park attendants, porters, bellboys, desk attendants, clerical assistants and housekeepers.

Depending on the establishment, you could ask at the front desk if work is available. I remember when staying in a small B&B in London a young chap came in and asked if there was any work. The next day, he had been given a job as a chambermaid and was serving me breakfast and making my bed. Larger establishments will most likely have a human resources department or else they can advise you of the recruitment agency they use.

Kitchen hands

Many find positions as kitchen hands, either washing dishes, pots and pans and/or preparing food. These positions don't necessarily need a qualification and are usually picked up by door-knocking.

Roadhouses and roadside diners

Roadhouses and roadside diners are places to stop, fill up with petrol, have a rest and something to eat. They are found all over the world on major freeways or as you approach or leave town. Sometimes they *are* the town.

The food on offer ranges from fast food to sit-down meals in a restaurant. These establishments often require staff as petrol attendants, mechanics, cooks, waiters, etc. Securing a position is usually a matter of asking over the counter if help is required.

As some of the roadhouses and roadside diners are remote, you may need transport to get to them each day. Extremely remote ones can offer some basic accommodation.

Waiting

Waiting on tables is a universal profession. The work available ranges from working in fast-food outlets and coffee shops to restaurants and private parties. There are also opportunities to work on cruise liners and in major resort areas.

Many find positions either by door-knocking or through specialist employment agencies. Those with silver-service skills may wish to contact cruise lines.

A set of full 'black and whites' are required and a waiter's friend (a bottle opener) will be required for positions. Some places do provide a uniform.

INFORMATION TECHNOLOGY

There is a huge demand for information technology (IT) professionals to fill contract positions around the world.

If you are an IT person, you will no doubt have access to a computer and the World Wide Web. Have a look at the following useful sites for contract employment around the world.

The on-line site of the *Freelance Informer* magazine has a searchable database with thousands of positions, which you can apply for on-line. There is useful information repeated from the magazine, including overviews of work opportunities (including skills in demand, for example SAP, and expected hourly rates) in areas of the world including Northern, Southern and Eastern Europe, Scandinavia, North and South America, South-East Asia, the Gulf and the Middle East, South Africa, Australia and New Zealand. Website address: www.freelanceinformer.co.uk

The website of **VNU Business Publications** has an extensive portfolio of IT publications including *Computer Contractor*, *PC Dealer* and *PC Week*. Website address: www.vnunet.com

This site is linked to www.JobWorld.co.uk which has thousands of current on-line permanent and contract positions available for IT professionals posted by recruitment agencies, as well as hundreds of vacancies posted by employers themselves.

You can browse by industry sector or search for a specific job or skill. Also look at:

Careermosaic: www.careermosaic.com

Monsterboard

Australia and New Zealand: www.monsterboard.com.au
Belgium: www.monster.be
Canada (in French and English): www.monster.ca
Netherlands: www.monsterboard.nl
United Kingdom: www.monsterboard.co.uk
USA: www.monsterboard.com

Positions can also be found through specialist information technology employment agencies. Look in the major newspapers where they advertise. Many of the accounting, banking and financial agencies have IT divisions. Refer to their contact details under 'Accounting, banking and financial services' earlier in this chapter.

NANNY, MOTHER'S HELP AND AU PAIR POSITIONS

These days the definitions of a nanny, mother's help and au pair are almost interchangeable. Basically they are all live-in positions involved with looking after children. Still, there are differences.

A *nanny* is usually formally trained or has extensive experience with children. She will undertake full-time (sole-charge) care of the children in the parents' absence. All duties will revolve entirely around the children and she should not have to undertake housework apart from what is related to the children, for example keeping their room tidy or washing their clothes.

A *mother's help* usually has no formal qualification, a little experience and can be young. As the name suggests, she helps the mother and often undertakes light housework as well as child-care duties.

An *au pair* is more often than not a traveller who is untrained and employed to assist the mother on a part-time basis. Usually the au pair's priority is to experience the culture of a different country and learn or refine the new language as she works for the family. The au pair industry, particularly in Europe and the USA, is regulated by government, therefore you can often enter a country under a 'cultural exchange visa' if you meet the stipulated criteria. This is not the case with nanny positions.

The child-care industry is dominated by females. (For this reason I have referred to child carers in the feminine.) There are, however, positions for males, and many families are happy to employ males, but I must stress that male carers can have a hard time finding a position. Europe is an exception.

The advantage of taking such employment is that positions are mostly live-in (though live-out positions as a 'daily' are available). A live-in position takes care of work and accommodation in one hit. The family provide you with a wage, your own room, full board, often use of a car and sometimes holidays abroad with the family.

Ensure your CV emphasises your child-care experience. Also, have at least two references (preferably child-care references) with contact details included. It is nothing for agencies and families to ring/email the other side of the world to check references. Some positions also require you to undergo a medical examination, so obtaining a clearance from your doctor is worthwhile. Criminal clearance from your local police is now becoming a necessary document.

Before you accept a position, you should have clarified: the hours you are expected to work and your time off; the duties required of you (How light is the light housework? How simple must the simple meals be?); your salary (including the day you will be paid, and how you will be paid); whether health insurance is included; and very importantly, how long the position is for (three, six or 12 months) and whether you need to sign a contract.

I would also suggest you find out as much about the family and the children as possible. Establish the number and ages of children you are prepared to look after. Do not take on newborns if you have no experience with them. Flexibility is also a consideration. If a parent is detained at work or both parents want to go out and require you to mind the children on your night off, you should be allowed to negotiate another night or hours off, or be paid extra for your services. Don't be afraid to discuss the situation with the parents or with the agency who placed you in the position.

Most positions can be found through specialist nanny employment agencies. A good agency should match you with a family and not just place you in a position. Once you are in a position they should offer assistance and support. Many agencies advertise in the newspapers, backpacker magazines or child-care magazines.

Many nanny employment agencies have links with other agencies in other countries and thus can help you with overseas positions. Some of the nanny schools also have a job placement section which can help you find positions overseas (after you have done a nanny course with them).

Australia

Australia offers the traveller live-in au pair and nanny positions. Look under 'Domestic Positions' in the Employment section of the *Sydney Morning Herald* on a Saturday, in which both families and specialist nanny and au pair placement agencies advertise.

Specialist nanny and au pair agencies also advertise in the Australian editions of *TNT Magazine* and *Aussie Backpacker*. You may also wish to look in *Sydney's Child*, a free monthly magazine available at libraries and child-related centres. It is aimed at parents but does include some nanny employment agencies.

Dial-an-Angel has 11 offices Australia-wide. You can contact its Lindfield office in Sydney for details of its other offices, or else have a look at its website.

Dial-an-Angel: www.dial-an-angel.com.au
Suite 1, 'The Colonnade'
2 Kohia Lane
Lindfield NSW 2070
Tel: (02) 9416 7511
Fax: (02) 9416 9400

Europe

EU and EEA nationals may work freely in EU and EEA member countries in child care. There are many agencies, particularly in the UK, which can place you in positions. It should be noted that European families are more accepting of males in child-care positions.

For those without an EU passport, au pair positions can be found under the 'cultural experience' mentioned previously.

Look in *The Lady* magazine (details below), where positions in the UK and throughout Europe can be found. Families advertise directly in this magazine as do specialist employment agencies. For agencies to help you find positions in Europe, refer to the United Kingdom listings below.

United Kingdom

Australians and New Zealanders are highly prized to join British families as nannies and mother's helps. There are positions available all year round, but families particularly look for nannies before and after the summer school holidays (September) when Australasian nannies have gone travelling and after Christmas when Australasian nannies go home.

Positions are available, particularly in London and in the 'home county' of Surrey, which is known as the 'nanny capital' of the UK. Positions also arise throughout the rest of the UK.

It is easy to secure a position on arrival in the UK through one of the vast number of specialist nanny employment agencies. Purchase a copy of *The Lady* magazine, a weekly publication in which nanny employment agencies and families (looking for a nanny) advertise. There are positions for the UK, Europe and other overseas destinations. You can purchase a copy from newsagents throughout the UK. If you are in another country ask your newsagent if they can get a copy, or contact the magazine directly for its subscription rates.

The Lady
39–40 Bedford Street
London WC2E 9ER, UK

Nanny employment agencies and families also advertise in *TNT Magazine*. Many UK nanny employment agencies have contacts with agencies in other countries or overseas offices and representatives to advise you on work opportunities. As Australians and New Zealanders are highly sought after for British families, many UK agencies have offices or representatives in these countries.

Bligh Appointments

Australia
Level 7, Dymocks Building
428 George Street
Sydney NSW 2000
Tel: (02) 9235 3699
Fax: (02) 9221 3480

United Kingdom
70 North End Road
London W14 9EP
Tel: (020) 7603 6123
Fax: (020) 7371 6898

Delaney International helps place candidates in positions in the UK. If candidates have an EU passport, Delaney International can also help with placements in European countries, for example Germany, Italy, France and Spain. Applicants should contact the main office for an application form and return the completed details together with an international reply coupon. For those in Australia and New Zealand, Delaney International has representatives who can start the ball rolling for you.

Although less in demand, male applicants for nanny, mother's help and au pair postions can be placed by Delaney International, providing they have good child-care experience.

Delaney International
Bramble Cottage
Thorncombe Street
Bramley
Surrey GU5 0ND, UK
Tel: (01483) 894 300
Fax: (01483) 894700

Australia
ACT: Mrs J. White, Tel: (02) 6286 4766
Qld: Mrs K. Jefferis, Tel: (07) 4039 1589
SA: Mrs H. Katzenberg, Tel: (08) 8431 0817
Vic: Mrs M. Drummond, Tel: (03) 9598 8871
WA: Mrs J. Innis, Tel: (08) 9581 6425

New Zealand
International Nannies   Tel: (09) 489 1026
A+ Nanny Network   Tel: (09) 424 1133

Dial-an-Angel can help young Australians with positions as nannies in the UK and as au pairs in the USA. See their details in the Australia listings above.

North South Agency offers candidates help finding au pair and nanny positions in the UK and throughout European countries, including Germany, Spain, Italy, Sweden, Switzerland and France.
28 Wellington Road
Hastings
East Sussex TN34 3RN, UK
Tel: (01424) 422 364
Fax: (01424) 715 120

USA

There are a number of au pair programs regulated by the US government allowing those between the ages of 18 and 26 the opportunity to join a family in the USA for one year as its au pair.
Au Pair America: the program includes organising the J-1 visa, placement with a family, full board and meals, and a weekly salary.

Au Pair America has associate offices throughout the world. Contact one for full details and costs of the program. You can access their addresses through a number of websites:
Au Pair America: www.aifs.com
www.aupairamerica.co.uk
www.campamerica.co.uk

Camp America is also an arm of AIFS, the American Institute of Foreign Study. Some offices include the following:

Australia
Southern Cross Cultural Exchange
Locked Bag 1200
14 Ranelagh Drive
Mt Eliza Vic 3930
Tel: (03) 9775 4711
Fax: (03) 9775 4971
Toll-free: 1800 500 501

New Zealand
Nannies Abroad
Private Bag MBE M400
Auckland
Tel: (09) 623 0126
Fax: (09) 623 7091

United Kingdom
37 Queen's Gate
London SW7 5HR
Tel: (020) 7581 7322
Fax: (020) 7581 7345

EF Education was founded in the Swedish university town of Lund over 30 years ago. It was originally called EF 'Europeiska Ferieskolan' (European Holiday Schools). This one small office has today grown into a multinational group consisting of nine companies which operate in over 30 countries.

EF Au Pair, one of the nine companies, has a program in which those aged between 18 and 26 can join an American family as its au pair. The program includes the J-1 visa for 12 months with an extra month for travelling, giving you a total of 13 months; a return flight to Australia or Europe; full room and board; a salary; and insurance coverage. There is also local support. For more details contact: www.ef.com

Australia
Level 3, 44 Miller Street
North Sydney NSW 2060
Tel: (02) 9460 0158
Fax: (02) 9929 5952

United Kingdom
Kensington Cloister
5 Kensington Church Street
London W8 4LD
Tel: (020) 7878 3560
Fax: (020) 7938 2940

NON-MAINSTREAM WORK

As you travel around the world, you will find you can create or just fall into opportunities. These opportunities are usually found by door-knocking, word of mouth, being innovative and creative, and taking opportunities and running with them. Here are a few non-mainstream suggestions for making extra funds.

Accommodation touting/running

This is where you frequent boat, bus and train stations and ask travellers (you can identify the travellers from their backpacks) if they are looking for accommodation. You then advise them of the advantages of staying at your accommodation, and give the price. If they are interested you then take them to the accommodation. For each new person you bring you receive a small commission.

Busking (or street performing) and entertainment

Buskers come in many forms (musicians, jugglers, mimers, singers, statues, etc.), and they can be all ages and work together or alone.

One thing to consider before you begin your act is whether or not you need a busking licence. If so, it is usually obtainable from the local council or town hall. Without the legal approval you will need to keep your eye out for the authorities.

Selecting your venue to make 'loads of cash' is crucial. You need to be accessible to the crowd with enough room for them to assemble. You need to find a place that does not block the thoroughfare or traffic. A big 'no-no' is infringing on another busker's turf. Many buskers share the same turf by allocating time slots. Don't forget your hat to pass around! The most popular places to perform include shopping malls, public transport stations, outside or near tourist attractions or at major festivals and events (you may need permission for this).

Profitable times can be during the morning, lunchtime and evening rushes. You could try busking outside popular attractions on a Sunday when many families go out for the day. Busking in the lead-up to and during popular events and festivals may also be fruitful.

Entertainers who wish to work on cruise liners should refer to the 'Cruise-line positions' section earlier in this chapter.

Film extra

The movie industy is thriving in a number of countries. Although you may not be 'discovered', being a film extra may bring in some extra cash, and you could get to meet some stars along the way.

There have been cases where people have been walking along the street and someone from a film comes up to them and asks if they would like to be in a particular film as extras. Of course, this isn't exactly a regular occurrence, so you are advised to contact directly some of the studios, such as Fox Studios in Sydney, Studio 91 in Tel Aviv, Israel, the BBC studios, London, or studios in Hong Kong, Los Angeles and elsewhere.

Some studios have an Extras Department which hires extras directly for films. Other Extras Departments will contact an extras acting agency for extras. You can find such agencies usually listed under 'Theatrical Agents' in the local telephone directory.

Fishing centres

There are many fishing centres around the world where job opportunities arise. Though many fishing boats are family owned and run, they may require deck hands and cooks. On shore they may need staff to unload and sort the catch. Mending nets and maintenance of the boats also needs to be taken care of. There may also be opportunities in the local canneries.

The best way to find work in fishing centres is to ask around. I do recall a friend once offered to help unload a catch from a small trawler in the Greek islands. He wasn't offered a position, but did receive a big fish which he cooked for mid-morning breakfast.

Modelling

If you are serious about becoming a model, obtain a portfolio and contact a specialist agency. For those wishing to make some extra cash, try contacting art schools which require nude and life models.

Offering your services

You could offer to provide domestic services, e.g. mowing lawns, painting, gardening or moving furniture. If you don't mind such work, you could advertise your services or go door-knocking.

Fellow travellers may be a good market: hairdressers could offer cheap haircuts; people who sew could offer mending services; masseuses could offer foot massages. You could set up a stall at a market and offer your services by giving massages, braiding hair, etc.

My friend I just told you about who helped the fisherman unload his catch also helped a restauranteur set up tables and chairs in preparation for the day's trade. My friend didn't get a job out of that either, but did score a free coffee and cake.

Pet walking and grooming

Don't laugh, I've seen people being dragged along by—I mean out walking—other people's dogs. If you like dogs and don't mind walking in all weathers, then you could try dog walking. I don't know how lucrative it is, but it could be a way to keep fit.

Washing and grooming pets may also be an option. I suggest you place your own advertisement on noticeboards, in newsagent windows or in local newspapers.

Pushbike and motorbike courier/dispatch rider

Companies often courier documents and parcels to other companies in the same city or further afield. They do this by ordering a courier from a courier company to make the delivery, usually in a hurry. These courier companies, in turn, require staff to do the delivering either by pushbike or motorbike, as these vehicles can manoeuvre through traffic much better than cars. As a traveller, you may not have a car anyway.

There are a number of agencies that require couriers. Some will provide you with a bike, helmet and uniform, while others will require you to have your own bike and helmet. You will need a full, clean motorbike licence to work as a motorbike courier. It is advisable to purchase a street directory so you don't get lost.

Selling souvenirs and duty-free goods

Innovative travellers buy souvenirs (jewellery, clothing, hats, woven rugs, indigenous art and crafts, etc.) and duty-free items (alcohol, perfume, cigarettes) to on-sell at a profit. Be careful not to trade in items with customs restrictions.

OFFICE SUPPORT

Office support includes filing, answering phones, clerical work, data entry, word processing, desktop publishing and design, all of which is undertaken by receptionists, secretaries and personal assistants.

Skills required include audio (dictaphone), shorthand, a typing speed of at least 50 to 60 words per minute or 10,000 to 12,000 keystrokes, and the ability to use a switchboard and a variety of the latest word-processing and graphics packages. Anyone with some or all of the above skills will find it relatively easy to obtain work.

'What if I don't type? Is there work for me?' Yes, you could find a clerical position, possibly doing photocopying or answering the switchboard.

To find office support work, look in the employment sections of newspapers. There are also many employment agencies including large international companies such as ADECCO, Office Angels, Drake International, Reed, Manpower and Select Appointments, which, if you are currently working for them, will send your details to another office for you (even in other countries if you are going overseas). This will save time having to re-register with them. Be prepared to have your typing, shorthand and spelling skills tested when you register.

Corporate dress is usually required for office positions, though this can depend on the dress code of the office. The agency should advise you about this. If they don't, you can dress up on the first day, see what everyone else is wearing and dress accordingly.

Australia is a very popular destination and many working holidaymakers find work in office support positions. Most work is in Sydney, where there is an abundance of employment agencies. These include the companies mentioned above, which have offices in most of the other large cities around Australia. Many agencies advertise in the major newspapers, the backpacker magazines (*Aussie Backpacker* and *TNT Magazine Australia*) and in the free *Nine to Five* and *City Weekly* magazines, which are handed out at city railway stations.

The **United Kingdom** is an extremely popular destination, and there are a huge number of specialist office-support employment agencies catering for employers who highly prize Australians, New Zealanders, Canadians and South Africans to work for them.

These employment agencies advertise in *TNT Magazine* and the free magazines *Ms London*, *Girl About Town*, *Nine to Five* and *Midweek*, which are handed out at the major London Tube stations.

The **Australasian Temp Company** is part of the Lampen Group. It helps candidates who have secretarial, desktop publishing, reception, telephone, data-entry and legal secretarial skills find temporary and contract positions. Website address: www.australasian-temps.co.uk

Australia
Level 5, BHP House
1 Castlereagh St
Sydney NSW 2000
Tel: (02) 9221 0900
Fax: (02) 9221 0500

United Kingdom
125–129 Cheapside
London EC2V 6LL
Tel: (020) 7500 1709
Fax: (020) 7500 2133

New Zealand

Auckland:
Tel: (09) 357 9800
Fax: (09) 357 9801

Christchurch:
Tel: (03) 374 9222
Fax: (03) 374 9223

Wellington:
Tel: (04) 472 4157
Fax: (04) 471 0958

Bligh Appointments

Australia
Level 7, Dymocks Building
428 George Street, Sydney
Tel: (02) 9235 3699
Fax: (02) 9221 3480

United Kingdom
70 North End Road
London W14 9EP
Tel: (020) 7603 6123
Fax: (020) 7371 6898

HW Group: www.working-holidays.co.uk
This address provides information on working holidays in the United Kingdom only.

Australia: www.hwgroup.com/au
Level 9, 66 Hunter Street, Sydney
Tel: (02) 9510 1444
Fax: (02) 9510 1440

Republic of Ireland
10 Lower Mount Street
Dublin 2
Tel: (01) 676 5000
Fax: (01) 676 5111

United Kingdom
Cardinal House, 39–40 Albermarle Street
Green Park, London W1X 4ND
Tel: (020) 7629 4463
Fax: (020) 7491 4705

If you have legal experience of at least one to two years, then contact **Learned Friends**:

Australia
Melbourne:
Level 5, 179 Queen Street
Melbourne Vic 3000
Tel: (03) 9642 3992

Sydney:
Level 7, 92 Pitt Street
Sydney NSW 2000
Tel: (02) 9232 5858

United Kingdom
Bride House
18–20 Bride Lane
London EC4Y 8DX
Tel: (020) 7583 3955

RETAIL

To find positions in retail, ask in the stores directly, contact the human resource department or apply to a specialist agency.

Work in this field is usually constant throughout the year, though extra staff are needed during sale times (mid-year, New Year, end of season, etc.). During the lead-up to Christmas, extra staff are taken on to cater for shoppers. Positions wrapping gifts can be found.

SKI CENTRES

There are many ski centres around the world. Wherever you find mountains and snow there is some form of snow sport going on.

There is an astounding variety of jobs available in ski areas, including:

- food and beverage: chefs, bar staff, waiting staff (including silver service), kitchen staff (dish washers, salad preparers, etc.) and fast-food service;
- hospitality: bartending, waiting, housekeeping (chalet staff), room service and bellhops;
- office: reception, reservations, word processing and payroll;
- retail: sales assistants and cashiers;
- ski rental: customer service; file, wax and mend skis;
- other: ski-lift operators, attendants and technicians, ticket sellers, nannies, medical staff, public parking attendants, snow-makers, groomers and shovellers, rescuers;
- ski and snowboard instructors.

A big advantage of working in a ski centre is that employers often include a free ski pass (after a certain length of employment) in your employment package.

Most travellers find work by on-the-spot door-knocking, which is often time-consuming.

My advice to you is to visit a travel agent for ski brochures on the specific area in which you wish to find work. Travel brochures are a very good source of information. They provide maps of the areas, showing where the ski fields are; the average snowfall; the season dates; the number of runs and ski lifts; snow-making facilities; amenities in the area; the nearest major centre where work may be found in the services associated with the ski fields (restaurants, nightclubs and ski rental stores, etc.); details of special events to occur in the area (when extra staff may be required) like World Cup events; locations and addresses of ski and snowboard schools; and an extensive list of accommodation including the type of accommodation, number of rooms and amenities offered and, most importantly, the accommodation contact details.

To show how the above information can work, consider Aspen, one of the USA's largest ski resorts. From a ski brochure, I noticed Aspen has four ski areas with over 100 bars and restaurants. There is also a large number of retail shops and a variety of accommodation available. That means there are many opportunities available in Aspen. Use the information in ski travel brochures to your advantage.

Ski Expos are also a good source of information. A walk around the stands can prove very fruitful. The managers of individual chalets or associated services are on hand to promote their products, and they are also the ones who do the hiring (or can provide details of who does) for each season. Speak to them about opportunities.

Approaching tour companies that provide ski packages may be an option. Again, have a look at the ski brochures. Ski magazines may also carry advertisements.

Those who work in the ski fields often return year after year. So how do they do it? Well, they have spent time there as a tourist and built up contacts. Many employers prefer to have their staff organised before the season opens. So calls for staff through advertisements in publications begin a few months before the season starts.

Many travellers turn up 'on-spec' in search of work. Your timing will be crucial and unfortunately it is hard to predict the exact time you should turn up. Ski brochures will give you the dates of each season, but it depends on the presence of the white stuff as to when the season really kicks off. If there is no snow, then employers will only need minimal staff. If there is a bumper snowfall, the story will be different.

Some travellers arrive a few weeks before the season starts to find a position. Others wait until after the season opens, as there are always workers who leave during the season. Some travellers think working in a ski centre will be one big party (and it can be) but it is also hard work. The hard work and cold climate can turn some travellers off.

A major hurdle for employees is that not all employers offer them accommodation. You will need to sort this out yourself.

The following website lists some 2,000 resorts in 37 countries, and many ski resorts have their own website which you could look at. Website address: www.goski.com

Northern hemisphere ski centres

The northern hemisphere ski season runs from November to March/April (sometimes longer). There are some areas, such as in the Alps and Norway, which offer year-round skiing.

CANADA
The major ski centres of Canada are found in Alberta, British Colombia and Quebec.
Alberta: Banff, Jasper, Kananaskis, Lake Louise, Marmot Basin, Sunshine.
British Columbia: Blackcomb, Big White, Fernie Valley, Panorama, Silverstar Mountain, Whistler. (Whistler has an employment village office to cater for the vast number of people who seek work in the area every season.)
Quebec: Mont-Tremblant, Mont-Sainte-Anne.

EUROPE, SCANDINAVIA AND ISRAEL
There are a number of countries throughout Europe and Scandinavia with ski centres.
Andorra
Austria: Innsbruck, Kitzbuehel, Lech, St Anton.
France: Chamonix, Courchevel, Les Arcs, Meribel, Tignes, Val d'Isere.
Italy: Dolomite Mountains.
Norway: Vos, Lillehammer.
Switzerland: Davos, Engelberg, St Moritz, Verbier, Zermatt.

Work opportunities as chalet staff are often advertised in *The Lady* magazine. You may wish to contact:

PGL Young Adventure needs qualified ski instructors for ski programs. See the 'Holiday camps' section earlier in this chapter.

Village Camps runs ski programs for children and require qualified ski instructors to work in its camps. Refer to its details under the 'Holiday camps' section earlier in this chapter.

Israel: Mount Hermon and Golan Heights. The best way to find work on the slopes in Israel is to go there and try your luck! The season runs from December through to April.

JAPAN
The island of **Honshu** has a number of resorts, particularly in the Chuba Sangaku area where the 1998 Nagano Winter Olympics were held. There are also resorts on the island of Hokkaido.

UNITED KINGDOM
There are five ski centres in the UK, which are all found in the Scottish Highlands.

The Glencoe Ski Centre is on the western side of the Highlands and is quite remote.

The Nevis Range Ski Centre is also on the western side of the Highlands. It encompasses Ben Nevis, the highest mountain in the UK. The Nevis Range is near Fort William, so if you do not find a position at the ski resort you may find work in this town.

The Cairngorm Ski Centre is in the centre of the Scottish Highlands. The nearest town is Aviemore, sometimes referred to as 'Aussiemore' due to the number of Aussies who find work there.

The Lecht Ski Centre is rather small and remote. The nearest town is Tomintoul.

The Glenshee Ski Centre is very remote. The nearest town is Braemar where the Highland Games are held every summer in the presence of Her Majesty the Queen.

Positions are often found by door-knocking, but some are advertised in *TNT Magazine* in London.

USA
There are a number of US states which have ski centres. These include:
Alaska: Alyeska.
California: Alpine Meadows, Heavenly, Mammoth, Squaw Valley.
Colorado: Aspen, Beaver Creek, Breckenridge, Copper Mountain, Crested Butte, Keystone, Steamboat, Telluride, Vail, Winter Park.
Idaho: Boise, Sun Valley.
Montana: Bozeman, Big Mountain, Big Sky.
New Mexico: Taos.
Utah: Park City, Snowbird.
Wyoming: Jackson Hole.

If you are a full-time student and would like to spend up to four months in the USA working in a ski field, Resort America, Camp Counselors USA and IEP all have programs available that will let you do this. For their contact details refer to the 'Holiday camps' section in this chapter and the 'Programs' section in Chapter 5.

OTHER SKI CENTRES
Don't forget other, smaller ski centres in **Russia** (Caucasus Mountains), **Slovakia**, **Slovenia**, **Bulgaria** and **Morocco**.

Southern hemisphere ski centres

The southern hemisphere ski season runs from June to September/October.

AUSTRALIA
Good skiing can be found in two Australian States, New South Wales and Victoria.
New South Wales: Thredbo, Perisher Blue, Smiggins, Mt Selwyn, Charlottes Pass.
Victoria: Mt Buller, Falls Creek and Mt Hotham.

The Australian ski season runs from June until September. Individual resorts begin advertising for staff in the major city newspapers around March/April. For available positions in the New South Wales ski fields you can contact:

Jindabyne Employment Service
Razerback Plaza
Gippsland Street
Jindabyne NSW 2627
Tel: (02) 6457 2190

NEW ZEALAND
New Zealand has ski centres on both the North and South islands.
   North Island: Mt Ruapehu (this is a volcano which has been active in recent years).
   South Island: Mt Cook, Mt Hutt, Treble Cone. Queenstown is the major ski centre for Cardrona, Coronet Peak and the Remarkables.

OTHER SKI CENTRES
Don't overlook smaller and/or lesser known areas.
   South Africa: Drakensberg Mountains.
   South America: Las Lenas and Bariloche in Argentina. Valle Nevado, Portillo and Termas de Chillian in Chile.

TEACHING
Teaching English

Teaching English has long been one way for travellers to live, work and play their way around the world. Most positions are in English conversational schools where students of all ages come to practise their 'conversational English'.

Before we get into this section, note that you will see a number of abbreviations with regard to teaching English. Terminology you will come across includes EFL (English as a Foreign Language), ESL (English as a Second Language), TEFL (Teaching English as a Foreign Language), CELTA (Certificate in English Language Teaching to Adults) and TESOL (Teaching English to Speakers of Other Languages).

It should be stressed that just because you can speak English, doesn't mean you can teach it. Many travellers have found this out when they have taken positions teaching English without a formal qualification.

Although positions for teaching English arise where no formal qualification is required, the majority of schools do require their teachers to hold a qualification. Most travellers opt to obtain either the internationally recognised University of Cambridge/Royal Society of Arts Courses (Cambridge/RSA) Certificate or the Trinity Certificate in Teaching English administered by Trinity College, Dublin. Either of these two certificates is highly regarded and is a prerequisite to teach in many schools around the world.

Both these certificates take four weeks of full-time intensive training to obtain. Part-time courses are available. If you have never taught before, don't worry—you will be introduced to the fundamentals of teaching, including lesson planning, classroom management and teaching skills, and accessing and obtaining resources and materials.

As well as theory lessons, you will undertake micro-teaching—classes using your fellow students as pupils. This will enable you to put into practice the theory you will be learning.

The certificate can be a little expensive to obtain, but it is recognised worldwide and with it you can expect to find a far greater number of professional teaching positions in countries around the world than without it.

There are many language schools, TAFEs and universities offering these two accredited courses on a regular basis. They will often advertise in major newspapers, stating course dates. The schools mentioned further on in this section also run these courses and can provide employment in their networks throughout the world.

There are three ways you can find work. Either arrange a job beforehand or, after arrival, approach schools directly for a full- or part-time position. The third way is to advertise your services via noticeboards, etc., offering one-to-one English tuition. Positions are usually available year-round, so you can start work any time. The exception is in Europe where around 90 per cent of jobs start in October/November with another intake of students in January.

Contact the schools mentioned below about obtaining qualifications and organising positions before you leave. These schools have websites which allow you to search and apply for a position on-line.

Berlitz is renowned around the world for the travel guides it produces. Berlitz also has over 350 Berlitz Language Centres worldwide. You need to apply directly to each centre for a position. I noticed you can access current vacancies and apply for them on-line through Berlitz's website: www.berlitz.com

EF Education was founded in the Swedish university town of Lund over 30 years ago. It was originally called EF 'Europeiska Ferieskolan' (European Holiday Schools). This one office has today grown to a multinational group consisting of nine companies in over 30 countries.

One of the companies, **EF English First**, employs trained English language teachers for its schools in various countries. The schools cater for students of all ages who wish to learn English in their own country.
EF English First: www.ef.com

Australia
EF House
5–7 Young Street
Sydney NSW 2000
Tel: (02) 9247 7668
Fax: (02) 9247 7691

Ecuador
Catalina Aldaz # 363
Y Av. Portugal 24
Quito
Tel: (02) 465 335
Fax: (02) 466 833

Lithuania
T. Kosciuskos 11
LT 2000 Vilnius
Tel: (02) 79 16 16
Fax: (02) 79 16 46

Poland
Smonia 8, P18
00375 Warsaw
Tel: (022) 826 8206
Fax: (022) 826 0871

China
Ying Li Fu Training Center
No 167, Tai Yuan Rd
Shanghai 2000 031 PR
Tel: (021) 6466 3478
Fax: (021) 6415 0076

Indonesia
Wisma Tamara Lt 4
Ruang 402, Jl. Jend. Sudirman Kav.

Jakarta 12920
Tel: (021) 520 6477
Fax: (021) 520 4719

Mexico
Londres 188, C.P. 06600
Col. Juarez, Mexico DF
Tel: (055) 14 3333
Fax: (055) 14 1362

Russia
15 Brestskaya 1st Street
5th Floor, 125 047 Moscow
Tel: (0502) 937 3883
Fax: (0502) 937 3889

USA
EF Centre Boston
1 Education Street
Cambridge MA 02141
Tel: (0617) 619 1000
Fax: (0617) 619 1001

For information on schools in Casablanca, Morocco, contact the EF Centre in Boston: www.ef.com *or* www.englishtown.com

International House has schools in some 30 countries of the world, including Argentina, Australia, Belarus, Brazil, the Czech Republic, Egypt, Estonia, Finland, France, Germany, Hungary, the Republic of Ireland, Italy, Lithuania, Macedonia, Malaysia, Mexico, New Zealand, Poland, Portugal, Romania, Russia, Singapore, South Africa, Spain, Switzerland, Turkey, Ukraine, the United Kingdom

and the United States. International House offers courses for people to gain the professional CELTA qualification. You can also find employment at one of their schools. Most of the recruiting for their schools is either done through the Staffing Unit, which is based in London, or on a local basis by affiliated schools. Its website has an extensive directory of International House schools. You can apply on-line for positions at this address: www.international-house.org
The Staffing Unit
International House
106 Piccadilly
London W1V 9FL, UK
Tel: (020) 7491 2598
Fax: (020) 7499 3708

While on-line, have a look at or contact the following:

A job section listing current positions from around the world can be found at www.tefl.net and you can apply for these positions on-line. There is also a monthly e-zine you can subscribe to for free.

There is an English Language Teacher Job Centre which you can access to see current job listings from around the world. You can apply for positions on-line. Website address: www.edunet.com

Another site provides a very useful overview of English-teaching job prospects and working conditions for specific world regions. Website address: www.english-international.com

Teaching English in Japan

Teaching English has long been the staple work opportunity for travellers to Japan. This is because many Japanese undertake English conversation lessons from a specialist English-language conversation school. The two largest English schools are Nova Corporation and Aeon (details follow).

There are two ways to find a position teaching English in Japan. Either organise a position before you go or approach schools directly after your arrival. There are a number of advantages to organising a position before you go—your visa, a position and accommodation are all arranged for you.

Aeon Corporation has over 220 English conversation schools throughout Japan.

It is preferred that teachers have the ESL/EFL teaching qualification but it is not obligatory. Some Japanese language is also useful but not mandatory.

Aeon Corporation: www.aeonet.com

Australia
Level 66, MLC Centre
19–29 Martin Place
Sydney NSW 2000
Tel: (02) 9238 2348
Fax: (02) 9238 2355

Japan
Tel: (086) 222 6378

USA
9301 Wilshire Boulevard
#202, Beverly Hills CA 90210
Tel: (0310) 550 0940

The **Nova Corporation** began as a single language school in Osaka, Japan, in 1981. Today, it has over 3,000 staff in around 350 private language schools throughout Japan. Each language school offers English language instruction to students of all ages who wish to learn English. Classes are small with three or four students per class with an emphasis on conversational English rather than reading and writing.

Most of Nova's teachers are hired outside Japan for full- and part-time positions. Full-time teachers are required to have a university degree, while part-time teachers do not necessarily need a qualification as full training is provided.

Nova helps you with the appropriate work visa, and offers the following: a contract position for one year; a competitive salary, furnished accommodation which is close to the school and which you will share with other teachers (this is a big plus for those travelling on their own); insurance; holiday pay; and all the assistance you need before and after your arrival and during your stay.

Nova Corporation: www.nova-group.com

Australia
Level 23, 141 Queen Street
Brisbane Qld 4000
Tel: (07) 3221 6991
Fax: (07) 3221 6992

Canada
1881 Yonge Street, Suite 700
Toronto, Ontario M4S 3C4
Tel: (0416) 481 6000
Fax: (0416) 481 1362

Japan
Head Office:
Midosuji Minami Building, 8F
2-3-2 Nishi Shinsaibashi
Chuo-ku, Osaka 542
Tel: (06) 213 4244
Fax: (06) 213 2544

Tokyo:
Harajuku Kariyonkan Building, 4F
1-8-9 Jingu-mae
Shibuya-ku Tokyo 151
Tel: (03) 3478 3475
Fax: (03) 3478 3222

United Kingdom
Carrington House, 126–130 Regent Street
London W1R 5FE
Tel: (020) 7734 2727
Fax: (020) 7734 3001

USA
Boston:
2 Oliver Street
Boston MA 02110
Tel: (0617) 542 5027
Fax: (0617) 542 3115

San Francisco:
601 California Street, Suite 702
San Francisco CA 94108
Tel: (0415) 788 3717
Fax: (0415) 788 3726

Teaching in the United Kingdom

Australian and New Zealand teachers are highly regarded in the United Kingdom. It isn't that there are not enough UK teachers to go around, but many have low morale and therefore do not make good emergency teachers, as do Australians and New Zealanders.

To undertake teaching in the UK you must be a fully qualified teacher holding a Bachelor or Diploma of Education. Unfortunately, regulations laid down by the European Union mean Australian and New Zealand qualifications are not recognised as being equivalent to European Union ones. This, however, will not make a difference if you find employment through a specialist teacher employment agency.

Specialist employment agencies can help find teachers relief casual positions in preschools, primary and secondary schools. Positions can be for a day, a week or a term. Most positions are found in England, either in Greater London or in Birmingham, West Midlands.

The school year runs from September to July and has three terms. Autumn term begins the first week in September (after the six-week summer holiday) and ends the third week in December. Spring term begins the first week in January until Easter, while summer term begins two weeks after Easter until the third week in July. There are also one-week breaks in the middle of each term known as 'half term'. Take note of term dates because there is no work available during the breaks, so it is a good time to take holidays of your own.

To find work, look in the *The Guardian* newspaper on a Tuesday and *The Times Education Supplement* (this does not come with *The Times*, it is a separate newspaper) on a Friday. Or contact one of the specialist teaching agencies listed. Many of them have offices in Australia, Canada, New Zealand and South Africa which you can contact for advice and to register with for work in the UK.

Many agencies also advertise in *TNT Magazine*, which is available free, throughout London.

BMG Associates has been helping teachers from the Commonwealth find temporary and contract positions throughout the United Kingdom since 1990. Contact one of their offices in Australia or New Zealand for helpful advice on getting ready to work as a teacher in the UK.

BMG Associates: www.bmgassociates.com.au

Australia
PO Box 2304
Fitzroy MDC, Vic 3065
Tel: (03) 9416 2333
Fax: (03) 9416 2399
Toll-free: 1800 813 149

New Zealand
61 Malvern Road
Mt Albert
Auckland 1003
Tel: (09) 849 3854
Fax: (09) 849 3854
Toll-free: 0800 803 854

LHR Educations helps place many Australasian teachers in primary and secondary teaching positions in Greater London.

LHR Educations: www.lhrteachers.co.uk

Australia
PO Box 1032
Warrnambool Vic 3280
Tel: (03) 5562 9426
Toll-free: 1800 240 130

New Zealand
PO Box 13
Pauanui Beach
Tel: (07) 864 7566

United Kingdom
2 Hammersmith Broadway
Hammersmith
London W6 7A1
Tel: (020) 8600 1300
Fax: (020) 8741 92800

Quality Teachers Ltd: www.quality-teachers.co.uk
9a High Street, Kings' Heath
Birmingham B14 7BB, UK
Tel: (0121) 441 1068
Fax: (0121) 441 4959

TECHNICAL, INDUSTRIAL, TRADES AND GENERAL LABOURING

Technical, industrial, trades and general labouring positions cover many professions in a variety of industries.

- technical: engineers, draughtsmen, architects, inspectors, tracers, etc.
- industrial: store people, forklift operators, drivers, stock takers, fitters, riggers, etc.
- trade: electricians, plumbers, carpenters, welders, boilermakers, etc.
- general labouring: labourers, process workers, dock hands, etc.

Work can be found in a range of industries, including manufacturing, mining, building and construction, transportation and warehousing. Work can also be found on cruise liners and yachts and at holiday resorts (such as the ski fields) to maintain and operate ski lifts, etc. Refer to the appropriate sections of this book for more details.

When you are seeking work, make sure you bring all of your trade certificates. Unfortunately, your qualifications may not be recognised in other countries, but work can still be found as an assistant in your field.

The large international employment agencies, such as ADECCO, Drake Overload and Manpower, have industrial sections which can place you in a variety of industrial positions.

Australia

The main cities in Australia, particularly Sydney, provide a vast number of jobs for those seeking general labouring and trade positions.

Your best bet is to register with the industrial section of an employment agency. Another possibility is to turn up at building sites and ask the person in charge if work is available or if they use an agency to supply staff.

United Kingdom

Many travellers find technical, industrial, trade and general labouring positions while in the UK. Employment agencies advertise in the *Evening Standard* newspaper and the traveller magazines, such as *TNT Magazine* and *Southern Cross*. For trades and general labouring positions:
John Gregory Labourers: Tel: (020) 8460 6420.
John O'Leary Building Contractors: Tel: (01730) 816 980
Engineers may like to contact:
Euro Elite plc: www.euroelite.co.uk
Western Australia House, 113–116 The Strand
London WC2 R0AA
Tel: (020) 7240 440
Fax: (020) 7379 7208
For packing, labouring and warehouse work:
Extraman: Tel: (020) 7373 3045
Olympic Industrial Staff: Tel: (020) 8840 0707

For engineering positions in **the Middle East:**
MH Matrix International Recruitment: www.mhmatrix.com

Australia
Level 9, Charles Plaza
66 King Street
Sydney NSW 2000
Tel: (02) 9262 4739
Fax: (02) 9262 5599

New Zealand
36 Omahu Road
Remerah
Auckland
Tel: (09) 524 6035
Fax: (09) 9524 6095

Engineers may like to contact aid agencies. Refer to 'Aid work' under the 'Volunteer work and programs' section later in the chapter.

TOURISM

Tourism includes a whole gamut of industries, including diving instructors, travel agents, tourist information centres, tour wholesalers, attractions, meetings and conventions, and tour guiding.

Diving instructors

If you are interested in learning to dive, or already are a diver, you could take this hobby one step further. There are work opportunities for divers with the appropriate level of qualification and experience.

You could find a position with a dive centre or resort, taking people out on diving trips. Or you could obtain work on a cruise liner taking diving groups out. This could be done virtually wherever there is water, but major diving regions include the Great Barrier Reef, the Caribbean, the Mediterranean, Pacific islands, the Maldives, Indonesia, the Philippines and Cozumel off the coast of Mexico. Other opportunities include teaching, water police, underwater oil-rig repair, underwater photographer, wreck diver and research diver.

To learn to dive or to progress to higher levels (for example divemaster), you will need to undertake training. When choosing a course, make sure it is internationally recognised, with locations all over the world, so no matter where you are, your certification card will be accepted and you will be able to go diving. There are a number of internationally recognised qualifications which you can obtain. These include:

NASDS (National Association of Scuba Diving Schools): www.nasds.com
NAUI (National Association of Underwater Instructors): www.naui.com
PADI (Professional Association of Diving Instructors): www.padi.com
SSI (Scuba Schools International): www.ssi.com

AUSTRALIA
Pro Dive runs PADI courses. If you are a qualified divemaster or instructor who has gained your qualification through Pro Dive, then you may wish to look into the 'Pro Dive Workaway Experience'. This is where Pro Dive says it can help place you in sought-after dive areas in Australia and around the world. Website address: www.prodive.com.au

There are a number of Pro Dive websites, including those for individual countries and popular diving areas. All provide information on the various dive courses available.

Tour guides/managers and coach drivers

This category can include site guides at cultural centres, tourist attractions, museums and national parks.

Tour companies require tour guides/managers to take charge of a tour group. They also need coach drivers with heavy vehicle licences and some mechanical experience (useful but not always necessary). Sometimes tour companies will advertise positions in major newspapers and backpacker magazines. I have noticed that some tour companies advertise in *TNT Magazine* in the UK during February/March seeking staff for the upcoming northern hemisphere summer.

You can also apply directly to a tour company's head office for a position. It is suggested you go to a travel agent and pick up the brochures for the tour company you would like to work for, then approach them directly. The websites of some tour companies (particularly jo-jos and backpacker tours) have an 'employment opportunities' section on their site. See Chapter 4 for the contact details of such companies.

Travel consultants

AUSTRALIA, UK AND IRELAND
Australia is a popular destination for the British and Irish, while the UK and Ireland are extremely popular with Australians.

Your local knowledge will make you employable in the many travel agencies catering for long-haul independent travellers. And when you get home you will find yourself in demand again. For help finding a temporary or contract position you may wish to contact:

AA Appointments

Australia
Level 25, Chifley Tower
2 Chifley Square
Sydney NSW 2000
Tel: (02) 9293 2833
Fax: (02) 9293 2821

United Kingdom
St Clare House
30–33 Minores
London EC3N 1BP
Tel: (020) 7480 7536
Fax: (020) 7265 1370

Travel Jobshop: www.traveljobshop.co.uk

Australia	*United Kingdom*
Level 2, 88 Pitt Street	Level 4, 16 Mortimer Street
Sydney NSW 2000	London W1N 7RD
Tel: (02) 9235 0231	Tel: (020) 7580 2131
Fax: (02) 9235 0379	Fax: (020) 7580 1293

Water sports

There are opportunities to turn your interest in water sports into a career. You will need a qualification to instruct and lead individuals and groups. Positions are available at holiday camps and major water-sport playgrounds.

TRANSLATORS

If you are bi- or multi-lingual, you might consider using your skills as a translator or interpreter. Such skills are needed in a variety of situations: at sporting events (e.g. Formula 1 where the teams require translations of the rules and regulations); when foreign dignitaries visit; at magazines, newspapers and other organisations when documents need to be translated; and at book publishers. Also, major tourist attractions (e.g. Euro Disney) may require people to make announcements in other languages or need bilingual staff in other capacities.

Berlitz Translation Services: You can access their website for current positions; address: www.berlitz.com/berlitz_corporate/employment_current_position.html

You may also wish to contact the **United Nations**.

VOLUNTEER WORK AND PROGRAMS

Most of us think of volunteer work as work done in foreign countries during and after civil wars and famines. We also may think that positions are reserved for medical professionals. The reality is that volunteer work also encompasses work as simple as collecting funds for a charity, offering your services for a day (or longer) at an orphanage or home for the elderly, or working in a charity shop. It can also encompass paying to participate on a conservation program.

Aid work

There are a number of international aid organisations. An aid agency's main aim is to assist individuals and communities during and after civil wars, environmental disasters (floods, cyclones, etc.) and epidemics. Assistance can be immediate and long-term.

Immediate assistance can involve medical help and providing food, warmth and housing to those in need.

Long-term assistance involves helping communities rebuild the infrastructure of their villages and towns. This can range from the construction and reconstruction of houses and other buildings and the restoration of services such as running water to helping to establish new crops and providing long-term medical programs, such as immunisation.

There are a number of areas where volunteers are required:
- medical: doctors, nurses, midwives, laboratory technicians and other allied health professionals;
- building: engineers and construction workers;
- other: administrators (accountants, receptionists) required to staff offices and administer funds, manage stock, hire local staff and organise what projects need to be done; cooks are also required.

It should be noted that you must be judged 'suitable' to undertake aid work as you will see and experience human tragedy first-hand. You will also be living in conditions that are not what you are used to.

Following are some aid agencies. Contact your nearest office (details available via their websites) for details of local, national and international volunteer work.

Amnesty International: www.amnesty.org

Care International: www.care.org

Medecins Sans Frontiers (MSF) is an emergency medical relief organisation. Besides health professionals (doctors, nurses, surgeons, anaesthetists, etc.), administrators and logistics staff are required.

MSF has offices in a number of countries around the world. To access their addresses have a look at the MSF website: www.msf.org

The **Missionaries of Charity** in Calcutta was set up by the late Mother Theresa to help the disadvantaged and impoverished peoples of India.

Missionaries of Charity
54A J.C. Bose Road
Calcutta West Bengal, India
Tel: (033) 244 7115

In 1859 some 40,000 soldiers lost their lives at a battle at Solferino. A young Swiss man, Henry Dunant, did what he could for the wounded. His efforts led to the founding of the **Red Cross**. The Red Cross provides help in two ways: the International Committee of the Red Cross (ICRC) provides aid to victims of war; the Federation of Red Cross and Red Crescent Societies aids victims of natural disasters.

Red Cross: www.redcross.org

The **United Nations** volunteer program began in 1970. Volunteers work under four sections: with governments who have technical skills shortages; in community-based initiatives; in humanitarian relief; and in the support of peace-building processes. Website address: www.unv.org

World Vision was founded in 1950 by Dr Bob Pierce, an American Christian evangelist. The organisation provides child-focused emergency relief. Website address: www.wvi.org

Most governments have aid projects. For instance, the USA has the Peace Corps (www.peacecorps.gov) and Australia has AusAID (www.ausaid.gov.au).

Archaeological digs

If you have ever dreamt of uncovering a prehistoric animal bone or a trinket thousands of years old, then here is your chance. You do not need to be an archaeological student to participate on a dig, you can pay to go on one.

As a volunteer, you will most likely spend your time either excavating in a trench with an experienced archaeologist or in the house/tent helping with cleaning, cataloguing and packing delicate objects. For information on archaeological digs:

Council for British Archaeology: www.britarch.ac.uk

This website lists upcoming fieldwork projects in Britain.

Archaeology Abroad (established 1972) is a publication issued three times a year (March, May and October) in which fieldwork and excavations are advertised. It is available on subscription from:
Honorary Secretary
Archaeology Abroad
31–34 Gordon Square
London WC1H 0PY, UK

You can access *Archaeology Abroad* through the Council for British Archaeology's website mentioned above.

The **Archaeological Institute of America** publishes an *Archaeological Fieldwork Opportunities Bulletin* every year which has a comprehensive listing of archaeological opportunities around the world. Contact the publishers:
Kendall/Hunt Publishing Co: www.kendallhunt.com
Order Department
4050 Westmark Drive
Dubuque, IA 52002, USA
Tel: 800 288 0810

Other websites to look at include:
European Archaeological Research Project: www.archeonet.cilea.it
ArchaeoLogic Communications: www.archaeologic.com/field_projects

For Australians wishing to experience archaeological fieldwork at Pella in Jordan you may wish to contact:
The Volunteer Co-ordinator
Pella Volunteers
NEAF (Near Eastern Archaeology Foundation), A14
University of Sydney
Sydney NSW 2006
Tel: (02) 9351 4151

Conservation programs

Conservation programs can be undertaken locally, nationally or internationally. Most conservation projects undertaken include tree planting, seed collection, construction and maintenance of walking tracks, erosion control, weed control, habitat restoration, heritage restoration and the monitoring of endangered flora and fauna. You could find yourself in some of the most beautiful and untouched parts of the world.

In most cases you will need to pay to go on a program. The price covers your meals and accommodation and usually project-related travel costs (though you will usually need to pay for your own fare to get you to and from the project site). Usually, you get to choose the program you want to go on from the programs available.

There are a number of conservation organisations that work together to offer international projects. Contact your nearest office for details of projects:
Australia
Australian Trust for Conservation: www.atcv.com.au
Europe: European Voluntary Service
Japan: The Department of Environmental Design
United Kingdom
The British Trust for Conservation: www.btcv.org.uk
USA
The South East Alaska Guidance Association
The California Conservation Corps
The Montana Conservation Corps

YACHT CREWING

Fancy spending your time island-hopping in the Caribbean or sailing around other exotic locations of the world? Well, many people have been able to do just that by either catching a lift, delivering a yacht, or by finding a position as a crew member on a boat.

Catching a lift

Wherever there is open water you will find some kind of yacht. The best way to find a lift is to frequent yacht clubs where yachts are moored and speak to the captains. Before you board, keep in mind that while, for you, a yacht may be just a means to get from A to B, for some yachties it is home, so make sure you first seek 'permission to board'.

You may like to place an advertisement on a yacht club's or sailing school's noticeboard stating that you are looking for a lift. Include where you would like to go and when. And don't forget a contact number.

Depending on the captain, you may find you either have to contribute to the running expenses of the yacht (including food) for the length of the trip (usually worked out per day), or you may be able to work your passage. Some people have saved thousands of dollars in travel costs by working their passage. Do note you may be required to pay a bond and you should find out about insurance for any mishaps at sea. Popular places to catch a lift include:

- Sydney for the Whitsundays in Queensland or to New Zealand;
- Darwin for Asia;
- Auckland Harbour for the Pacific and the USA;
- Balboa (Pacific Ocean end) or Port of Cristobal (Atlantic Ocean end) of the Panama Canal;
- any of the Caribbean islands, particularly Antigua (English Harbour), Jamaica (Montego Bay) and the Isle of Martinique;
- Gibraltar: at the mouth of the Mediterranean, this is often a stop-off point for yachties to pick up supplies after crossing the Atlantic;
- Nice and Monte Carlo: in the Mediterranean, these are very popular;
- any of the Greek islands.

Many yachties spend the northern hemisphere summer sailing around the Mediterranean, then cross the Atlantic Ocean (which can take around six weeks) for the Caribbean, where they island-hop between September to April.

If you are worried that you don't have any experience, you may wish to undertake a sailing course to learn the basics.

Finding a position

There are many who 'drop out' and like to spend their time in exotic locations. Some either own their own yachts or charter them. Depending on the size of the vessel, there can be positions onboard. These include: captains, mates, engineers, chefs, cooks and stewards/stewardesses.

Work can also be found during times in 'dry dock', cleaning and scrubbing hulls, painting, re-fitting, mending sails, etc.

Besides speaking to captains and leaving advertisements on noticeboards (see 'Catching a lift', above), positions can be found by contacting a recruitment agency.

There are a number of agencies that can link crew (from novices to professionals) with captains/owners of boats who require staff or a boat to be delivered. Most of these agencies have websites listing positions which you can apply for on-line.

Crewfinders International Inc: www.crewfinders.com
404 SE 17th Street
Fort Lauderdale, FL 33316, USA
Tel: (0954) 522 2739
Fax: (0954) 761 7700

Crewseekers International: www.crewseekers.co.uk
Hawthorn House, Hawthorn Lane
Salisbury Green
Southampton S031 7BD, UK
Tel/Fax: (01489) 578 319

Nauti Crew Delivery and Crewing Agency:
www.whitsunday.net.au/nauti.crew.htm
Whitsundays Qld 4802
Australia
Tel/Fax: (07) 4948 2555

Index

accommodation 31
  short-term 32
  long-term 35
  pre-book 31
Africa
  travel 50
  work 99
Air 39
Antarctic, the
  travel 52
Australia
  travel 53
  work 100
B&Bs 34
backpack, choosing a 18
bank accounts 8, 30
camping grounds 35
Canada
  travel 55
  work 105
care work 145
Caribbean, the
  work 106
cars, vans and other vehicles 47
  buying/selling 48
  hiring of 47
  lift sharing 48
Central and South America
  travel 57
  work 107
check-in 26
check-up (medical) 11
cash 8
checklist 24
college campuses 35
courier flights 41
credit card 7
criminal clearance 16
Curriculum Vitae (CV) 16
customs 28
cycling 49
departure tax 26
discount cards 13
dorm living 32
dual nationality 2
duty-free 27

Egypt and Israel
  travel 59
  work 99
Email 13
employment agencies 92
Europe, Scandinavia and the Commonwealth of Independent States
  travel 60
  work 109
flat and house share 36
foreign exchange 6
frequent flyers 16
hitching 43
holiday apartments 35
holiday insurance and medical care 10
hostels 32
hotel chains 35
Indian sub-continent
  travel 63
  work
international driver's licence 12
Republic of Ireland
  travel 69
  work 112
Israel
  work 112
Japan
  travel 64
  work 116
Jo-jos and backpacker tours 46
kibbutz 113
live-in positions 37
Mediterranean, the
  work 119
Middle East, the
  work 119
mobile phones 14
money 6
moshav 115
National Trust 15
New Zealand
  travel 64
  work 121
Oceans, the

  travel 66
  work
passport 2
power of attorney 12
prepaid phonecard 14
programs 85
  agriculture 87, 134
  au pair 85
  holiday camps 87
  JET 117
reciprocal medical arrangements 10
scanners 26
South-East Asia and China
  travel 67
  work 122
sponsorship 89
tax number 30
tax obligations 97
travel 38
  alone 74
  country/area options 49
  options 39
  safe 75
  should you pre-purchase 38
  well 77
travel clubs 15
  Australian 101
  United Kingdom 126
travellers' cheques 6
United Kingdom and Republic of Ireland
  travel 69
  work 113
United States of America
  travel 72
  work 128
vaccinations 77
visas 3
water 49
will 12
Work
  cash 89
  options for finding 91
working holidays 84
world area map 82